International
Library of the
Philosophy of
Education

**John Dewey
reconsidered**

International
Library of the
Philosophy of
Education

General Editor

R. S. Peters

Professor of Philosophy of Education
University of London
Institute of Education

John Dewey
reconsidered

Edited by

R. S. Peters
Professor of Philosophy of Education
University of London
Institute of Education

Routledge & Kegan Paul
London, Henley and Boston

First published in 1977
by Routledge & Kegan Paul Ltd
39 Store Street,
London WC1E 7DD,
Broadway House,
Newtown Road,
Henley-on-Thames,
Oxon RG9 1EN and
9 Park Street,
Boston, Mass. 02108, USA
Set in IBM Baskerville
by Express Litho Service (Oxford)
and printed in Great Britain by
Lowe & Brydone Printers Ltd
Thetford, Norfolk

British Library Cataloguing in Publication
Data

John Dewey reconsidered. — (International
library of the philosophy of education).

1. Dewey, John — Addresses, essays, lectures
I. Peters, Richard Stanley II. Series
191   B945.D44   77–30006

ISBN 0 7100 8623 7

Contents

Contributors

Jerome Bruner
Watts Professor of Psychology
University of Oxford

Eileen Caudill
Research Assistant
Penn University

Antony Flew
Professor of Philosophy
University of Reading

Martin Hollis
Senior Lecturer in Philosophy
University of East Anglia

Anat Ninio
Teaching Fellow in Psychology
The Hebrew University of Jerusalem

R. S. Peters
Professor of Philosophy of Education
University of London Institute of Education

Anthony Quinton
Fellow of New College
University of Oxford

Alan R. White
Ferens Professor of Philosophy
University of Hull

General editor's note

There is a growing interest in philosophy of education amongst students of philosophy as well as amongst those who are more specifically and practically concerned with educational problems. Philosophers, of course, from the time of Plato onwards, have taken an interest in education and have dealt with education in the context of wider concerns about knowledge and the good life. But it is only quite recently in this country that philosophy of education has come to be conceived of as a specific branch of philosophy like the philosophy of science or political philosophy.

To call philosophy of education a specific branch of philosophy is not, however, to suggest that it is a distinct branch in the sense that it could exist apart from established branches of philosophy such as epistemology, ethics, and philosophy of mind. It would be more appropriate to conceive of it as drawing on established branches of philosophy and bringing them together in ways which are relevant to educational issues. In this respect the analogy with political philosophy would be a good one. Thus use can often be made of work that already exists in philosophy. In tackling, for instance, issues such as the rights of parents and children, punishment in schools, and the authority of the teacher, it is possible to draw on and develop work already done by philosophers on 'rights', 'punishment', and 'authority'. In other cases, however, no systematic work exists in the relevant branches of philosophy — e.g. on concepts such as 'education', 'teaching', 'learning', 'indoctrination'. So philosophers of education have had to break new ground — in these cases in the philosophy of mind. Work on educational issues can also bring to life and throw new light on long-standing problems in philosophy. Concentration, for instance, on the particular predicament of children can throw new light on problems of punishment and responsibility. G. E. Moore's old worries about what sorts of things are good in themselves can be brought to life by urgent questions about the justification of the curriculum in schools.

There is a danger in philosophy of education, as in any other applied field, of polarization to one of two extremes. The work could be practically relevant but philosophically feeble, or it could be philosophically sophisticated but remote from practical problems. The aim of the new International Library of the Philosophy of Education is to build up a body of fundamental work in this area which is both practically relevant and philosophically competent. For unless it achieves both types of objective it will fail to satisfy those for whom it is intended and fall short of the conception of philosophy of education which the International Library is meant to embody.

John Dewey was a philosopher who pre-eminently tried to relate his philosophy to practical concerns. He was also best known for his philosophy of education. It is therefore appropriate that an attempt to reappraise both his general philosophy of man and society as well as his philosophy of education, which was intimately connected with both, should appear in the International Library of the Philosophy of Education.

This collection of papers was made possible by the generosity of the John Dewey Foundation who gave a grant to the University of London Institute of Education to put on a course of public lectures on John Dewey's philosophy, in the hope that the reading and study of the works of John Dewey would thereby be encouraged. After the lectures there were countless requests that they should be made available in published form to be read and examined at more leisure. This collection is a response to such requests.

R.S.P.

Inquiry, thought and action: 1
John Dewey's theory of knowledge
Anthony Quinton

1 Introduction

Pragmatism began as a theory of meaning. It is often dated from the publication in 1878 of Peirce's article 'How to make our ideas clear', in which the meaning of an idea is identified with its 'practical bearings', that is to say the difference its being true would make in terms of experiencable consequences in the future. It is perhaps most familiar as a theory of truth, especially in the form given to it by William James for whom the true is what it is good, expedient or satisfactory to believe.

But pragmatism is also a theory of knowledge and was so from the beginning. In two articles that appeared in W. T. Harris's *Journal of Speculative Philosophy* as early as 1868, its second year ('Questions concerning certain faculties claimed for man' and 'Some consequences of four incapacities'), Peirce argues elaborately and ingeniously against what he calls Cartesianism, the idea that knowledge should be constructed from intuitively self-evident beliefs in minds that have been cleared of all habitual assumptions by a process of universal doubt.

As Peirce himself says, 'most modern philosophers have been, in effect, Cartesians', and this is true of British philosophers in particular. Locke's view that all knowledge must be derived from the intuitive deliverances of sensation and reflection, if empirical, and from intuitive awareness of conceptual connections, if it is not, has been the common conviction of the central tradition in British epistemology that stems from him, through Berkeley and Hume and then John Stuart Mill to Russell and such Russellian theorists of knowledge of more recent times as Price and Ayer. What is more, the varying accounts the members of this tradition have given, on their shared Cartesian basis, of our knowledge of the material world, the minds of ourselves and others, of the past and of the laws of nature, have remained, until the last few decades at least, the centre of constructive philosophical interest and are still today the initial core of philosophical teaching.

Yet until the publication of W. B. Gallie's *Peirce and Pragmatism* in 1952 there was no British discussion of Peirce's anti-Cartesianism and even now such currency as its conclusions have is perhaps more attributable to the influence of the rather similar account of the 'basis-problem' in Popper's *Logic of Scientific Discovery* than to Peirce's presentation of it.

James's epistemological ideas are, indeed, familiar in the developed form of his radical empiricism through the fact that Russell was converted to them. In his essay on 'The nature of acquaintance' in 1914, Russell criticized James's neutral monism from the point of view of his conviction that in perception a mental subject is related to a physical object that is totally different in nature from it. By 1918 with 'The philosophy of logical atomism' and, even more, by 1922 with the *Analysis of Mind*, Russell's conversion to James's way of thinking was complete. But this was hardly a conversion to pragmatism, even to pragmatist epistemology, from which James's doctrine, with its close affinities to the ideas of Mach and, on a natural reading, Hume, is really a deviation.

The chief continuator of Peirce's anti-Cartesianism was John Dewey. He combined it with James's emphasis on the acquisition of knowledge as an active and exploratory process, rather than a kind of passive contemplation, with the view, present in much pragmatism, but particularly emphasized by Schiller, that the conceptual instruments of thought are human constructions not independent Platonic existences and, third, with an insistence on the social character of knowledge that is to be found in Peirce, to produce a distinctive theory of knowledge that has a remarkable coherence of tone despite the breadth of its scope and, it must be admitted, the frequent turgidness and amorphousness of its expression.

It is this theory of knowledge of Dewey's that I shall be discussing today. I find all of its main contentions at least suggestive even if, in the form in which Dewey presents them, they are open to much criticism. In general, those constituents of the whole for which Dewey is himself chiefly responsible are, I shall argue, more acceptable as regards what they deny than as regards what they positively affirm. It is still odd that a body of extensive critical discussion that addresses itself to such fundamental aspects of the traditional British theory of knowledge should have secured so little attention here.

2   The four themes of anti-intellectualism

A term is needed to pick out Dewey's theory of knowledge from pragmatism in general. His own preferred designation, instrumentalism, is not altogether satisfactory since it concentrates too much on one part of the whole. It is perhaps best characterized in negative terms as anti-intellectualism. It can be set out by listing its four main points of conflict and disagreement with the familiar Cartesian tradition.

1   In the first place where the Cartesian seeks to base all knowledge on absolutely certain beliefs, on somehow self-evident items of intuitive knowledge, the anti-intellectualist contends that all our beliefs are fallible and corrigible. In consequence the task of epistemology is not to give an account of secure and certified knowledge but rather of rational and warranted belief. In general, the beliefs on which we act are not established certainties. The demand for established certainty is exaggerated and utopian. We must be content with warranted assertibility which falls short of absolute and ideal truth. It is in the spirit of this conviction that Dewey puts himself forward as a theorist of *inquiry* rather than a theorist of *knowledge*.

2   Second, the anti-intellectualist sees the knower or inquirer, the pursuer of rational and warranted belief, as an active being, an experimenter, not as a contemplative theorist. It is in this connection that Dewey launches his polemics against the 'spectator theory of knowledge'. Our rational beliefs about the world in which we live and act are not the result of a kind of Augustinian illumination, passively received, and then privately worked up and systematized in the recesses of our own minds. They are, rather, the outcome of deliberate, experimental interaction with our environment. Furthermore the intellectual apparatus which we bring to this

cognitive encounter with the world is not something imposed on us by the pervading structure of the world outside. Our conceptual equipment is a body of instruments that we have devised and constructed ourselves, under the pressure of our own needs and purposes.

3   Third, the subject or possessor of knowledge or warranted belief is not, in the manner of intellectualism, a pure mind or consciousness, a Cartesian *res cogitans*. It is, in Dewey's view, an intelligent organism, an embodied thing, animated by primarily bodily purposes, and forming its beliefs about the world around it through bodily, physical interaction with it. Manipulation is at least as crucial to the formation of rational beliefs as more or less detached inspection.

4   Fourth and finally, the anti-intellectualist sees the pursuit of rational belief as an essentially social undertaking, in contrast to the subjective isolation of the Cartesian knower, exposed as he is to various kinds of sceptical desperation. Knowledge or rational belief is a social product, an accumulation of common intellectual property, made up of what Dewey likes to call 'funded experience' and on which all may draw.

In short, the intellectualist sees knowledge as something absolutely certain, which is contemplatively seen, by a mind that is at most contingently embodied, working on its own. For Dewey's anti-intellectualism what is sought is rational and corrigibly fallible belief, actively achieved, even made or constructed, and with the aid of conceptual instruments of human design, by an intelligent but embodied organism that is a natural part of the world it seeks to know, engaged on this undertaking as a collaborating member of a society of intelligent organisms of the same kind.

3   Fallibilism

Let us consider the first theme, that of fallibilism. Intellectualism, particularly in its Cartesian and intuitionist form, defines knowledge as conclusively justified true belief and maintains that all rational belief must rest on knowledge thus defined. The anti-intellectualist is opposed to the suggested definition of knowledge as utopian and even superstitious but does not so much attack it by direct argument as simply replace it by a conception of knowledge held to be more realistic and useful.

In effect, that is to say that we should not bother ourselves with absolute certainties since they are not to be had and, fortunately, are not needed. What, he asks, is knowledge for? Primarily, persistingly and essentially for the sake of action. What we require is rational belief about the consequences of various alternative actions it is within our power to take. In being essentially practical, it is also essentially forward-looking and predictive and all such prediction is fallible.

In a way there is nothing here with which Cartesians generally, and Cartesians of an empiricist variety in particular, need quarrel. If absolute certainty is insisted on as a defining condition of knowledge then it will turn out that very little is known. Specifically what is truly known is whatever is intuitively necessary, whatever is in some way empirically self-evident and incorrigible, in other words the immediate deliverances of sensation and introspective self-consciousness, and whatever can be deduced from premises of either of these sorts by means of rules of inference corresponding to intuitive or demonstrated necessary truths. On this view most of what is of practical interest for man as an active being will not be known. Cartesian empiricists will agree that with regard to the material world, the past, the minds of others and the laws of nature, we can have at best rational belief, for all propositions about these are neither intuitive nor demonstrable. For the most part they will be the conclusions of non-deductive inference which are at best confirmed and never certified by the evidence on which they rest. (Knowledge of the past by memory is not inferential, of course, but it is as fallible as if it were and thus as little entitled to description as knowledge proper.) No one could be more emphatic that the beliefs of science and common sense are not truly knowledge than Russell, unless it were Hume.

But, if the Cartesian tends to admit that very little of what we believe, and, in particular, practically none of the beliefs which directly guide our actions, are truly known in his sense of the word, he still insists that the little that is truly known is of the utmost importance. This is because of his second thesis that there can be no rational belief that is not derived from knowledge proper.

Dewey does not, so far as I know, attack this thesis directly but I believe it to be mistaken. It is commonly presented as the only alternative to a coherence theory of knowledge in which every belief owes its justification to its inferential relation to other beliefs (a position something very like that to which Peirce was driven by his rejection of intuitionism). This view leads to an infinite regress which presents every appearance of being vicious. Beliefs cannot simply pass justification from one to another without, so to speak, their having some initial stock of justification from another source.

But such a coherence theory is not the only alternative to intuitionism. The fact that all beliefs that derive whatever justification they have to non-deductive inference from other beliefs are less than absolutely certain does not entail that all beliefs that are less than certain are inferential in the way described. In other words it is not clear that all rational, but less than absolutely certain, belief must be derived from beliefs that are absolutely certain and incorrigible.

It is possible to hold that there are foundations to knowledge, or, more precisely, relative foundations, which, while not absolutely certain, are nevertheless rationally believed, not on the strength of other beliefs that inferentially support them but on the strength of experiences that do not certify them but simply render them more worthy of acceptance than rejection. Just this is true, I believe, of the propositions about perceived material things and the remembered past that are the apparent, rather than theoretically alleged, foundations of our empirical beliefs about matters of fact.

If this view is accepted it is not necessary to suppose that our beliefs about the material world as we commonly take ourselves to perceive it are really inferences from antecedent beliefs about our sense-experiences or again that our beliefs about the recollected past are inferred from antecedent beliefs about memory-data.

Although these basic empirical beliefs about the perceived material world and the recollected past are not initiated or wholly dependent for their justification on inference from other, more certain beliefs, they are, nevertheless, subject to inference, in so far as they can be further confirmed by other beliefs of the same corrigible but credible status, in the light of equally corrigible general beliefs about the way in which the constituents of the material world behave and hang together. Equally, of course, they may, despite their initial credibility, be undermined by inference from a preponderating body of comparable beliefs.

This brings us back to the definition of knowledge in terms of absolute certainty. What this defining condition in fact comes to is that a proposition can be known only if it would be an evident or demonstrable contradiction to deny it or if it follows from the fact that it is believed that it is true. In either of those circumstances there would be some kind of logical absurdity in the supposition that the belief in question might be false. But without going to the length of blithely re-defining knowledge as well-confirmed belief, it might be felt that that is altogether too stringent an account of certainty.

The certain, it could be suggested, is not that which it is somehow logically absurd to doubt, but that which there is no reason to doubt; that which rationally ought not to be doubted, not that which logically cannot be. Now in these terms although no basic empirical proposition may be certain as prompted by experience alone, it may acquire certainty from the addition to that confirmation of the support of other equally fallible beliefs. Certainty, on such a view, is something ascertained, not something initially given. But it could be what we ordinarily understand by the word.

I conclude, then, that the Cartesian does define knowledge too restrictively and that he is mistaken in thinking that its uninferred empirical basis must be incorrigibly certain. But such ideal certainty is not really essential to knowledge and ordinary certainty is attainable for basic empirical beliefs even if they are not endowed with it by the experiences that directly prompt them. In rejecting the Cartesian's definition of knowledge Dewey goes too far in the opposite direction and, in his emphasis on the fallibility of most practically important beliefs, says nothing that an empirically minded Cartesian could not accept, while failing to engage with their real mistake: the assumption that the foundations of knowledge must be logically immune from error.

4   Instrumentalism

The focus of Dewey's epistemology is his attack on the spectator theory of knowledge on behalf of instrumentalism or experimentalism. At a certain level of generality the idea that knowledge is actively and purposively sought, not just passively received, is likely to secure acceptance without much difficulty. It might indeed be said that our acquisition of knowledge or rational belief is neither wholly active nor wholly passive. Surely a certain amount of what we know or reasonably believe just gets borne in on us and does not take the form of answers methodically secured to antecedently formulated questions. The process by which I have come to know that I do not like the taste of liquorice, that my colleague is in a rather irritable state today or that a friend's wife has put on a good deal of weight, does not deserve to be dignified with the description 'inquiry'.

In very general terms like these there is plainly much to be said on behalf of an active attitude in the knowledge-gathering operation. In the tone of an epistemological Polonius one could urge that if knowledge is actively sought it will be both better founded and a great deal more copious than if it is merely allowed to accumulate in a passive manner. It is this active attitude, after all, that is the most fundamental mark of distinction between science and common sense; for whatever else it may be, science is at least a deliberate and methodical effort to answer questions about the nature and connection of things. If beliefs are just allowed to form by a kind of natural accretion they are perhaps peculiarly likely to be incorrect. To produce a final bromide: one generally does something better if one attends to what one is doing.

At the same level of rather bland generality is Dewey's insistence that the process of inquiry is prompted and set in motion by men's practical needs, that knowledge is for the sake of action. Here again, one may readily admit that a great deal of knowledge is of this kind, perhaps most of the knowledge that most people have. But there is such a thing as pure curiosity, as distinct from the curiosity which arises from a suspicion that something may have hitherto unknown properties that call for action, perhaps of a pre-emptive kind, and, one has to add, from the impure curiosity of the inquirer who has to find something out in order to pass an examination or retain a job, however practically indifferent he may be to the content of what he is seeking to find out. Polonius is waiting in the wings once again at this point, bursting with the information that many things that people have been motivated to discover by the love of knowledge for its own sake have later turned out to be of the highest significance for practical human purposes. One may sympathize with Dewey's anxiety to make philosophy serviceable to men in general in the concerns of everyday life without feeling obliged to make out its credentials in this respect in all its aspects.

Instrumentalism takes on a more concrete and definite character in the form of the thesis that the materials of belief, the concepts in which beliefs are formulated, are human constructions and not imposed on men by the nature of things. This thesis is directed against intellectualism of a Platonic kind which takes the conceptual materials of our thought to be somehow imposed on us by the nature of things. Our conceptual apparatus, on this view, reflects, to the extent that it is adequate for its task, the structure of an objective and timeless realm of essence. Dewey was always hostile to Platonism on more or less democratic or egalitarian grounds. He took it to be the attitude to knowledge appropriate to a slave-owning society in which true rational men or citizens did not soil their hands with the work of the world but sequestered themselves for purposes of abstract, theoretical contemplation. But there is a certain vulgarity about this opinion. Mathematics and metaphysics are not dirty work, except in the marginal forms of computer engineering and sorcery, but that does not mean that they are not work, that they are not fields of active, answer-seeking effort, typically, I should suppose, more so than the routine discharge of practical tasks.

The active, imaginative invention or construction of concepts is most evident at the level of scientific theorizing. The

9

theorist's intellectual fertility does not show itself only in bringing familiar concepts together in previously unformulated beliefs. It is also present in the devising of new concepts that are not part of the common stock of thought and discourse: elasticity of demand, deep grammatical structure, the quantum of energy, the correlation coefficient.

Concepts of this kind differ from more familiar ones like red or square or tree or dog in that they have a history, a known history, that is to say, providing a date at which they were first introduced and the name of their first introducer. But two points need to be made here. The fact that a new concept was introduced into discourse at a particular time by a particular person does not mean that it is strictly an invention. The conceptual innovator may be just as well described as having brought off a feat of discovery. The actual or possible property or relationship that he succeeds in bringing to human consciousness may well have already been exemplified in the world, even if no one before him was aware of the fact. Indeed, if the new concept is to be of any use in the formulation of true beliefs, what the concept expresses must, in most cases, have been, or be going to be, actually exemplified. (The point of the qualification is to allow for concepts of ideal or limiting cases: the perfectly elastic fluid, the ideal gas, the economy in perfect equilibrium.) The conceptual innovator, in other words, must have one foot on the earth.

Second, although the fact of historic innovation may show some concepts to be the outcome of acts of imaginative creation, those concepts will be theoretical and sophisticated ones like the examples I gave. The ordinary notions with which they are contrasted, the everyday descriptive apparatus, would seem to be a piece of common human property of unhistoric antiquity and unhistoric immunity to reform and change. One rather obvious piece of evidence for this view is the translatability of ancient or geographically remote languages into the language we speak ourselves.

It is, of course, true that there are limits to translation. I am thinking here not of the problems raised by Quine but of the problem posed by Homer's 'wine-dark sea'. Even the most elementary and familiar concepts have a sort of history and we may reasonably suppose them to have emerged as part of the natural evolutionary development of mankind. That point of view undermines the old idea of a universal and identical human reason to be found in Aristotle and the Stoics and defended by Kant on the ground of the universal validity of logic. It seems reasonable to suppose that our conceptual apparatus is not a direct reflection of the nature and structure of the world but the result of an interaction, worked out in an evolutionary way, between the world and two things located in us: our perceptual equipment, on the one hand, and our needs and interests on the other.

The view of Platonic intellectualism, that our conceptual apparatus directly reflects the structure of the world, does not have as its only alternative the idea that our conceptual apparatus is a wholly free construction, imposed by us on the indefinitely plastic tissue of our environment. Between biscuits and clear homogeneous soup is minestrone. We can allow ourselves, that is to say, our perceptual equipment and our needs and interests, an important measure of free initiative in the formation of concepts without supposing ourselves to be absolutely free in this matter. The initiative in question is to select, from all the possibilities of comparison or similarity-finding that are present in the world, those that our perceptual equipment enables us to register, those which present themselves to the close attention that is excited by need and interest and those, finally, which while not thrusting themselves on perception nor directly ministering to an interest, allow for the conveniently brief formulation of laws or are, as one might say, explanatorily fertile.

The mind or knower, then, can be admitted to be conceptually creative without denying that the conceptual outfit it creates is some kind of reflection of the world; for surely, if it did not in some way reflect the similarities and differences to be found in the world it would be descriptively useless. If our thinking is to be communicable from one person to another the words in which they express it must, where the same, apply to much the same things. We must share dispositions to classify things together and to distinguish them. If that is to happen things classified together must strike us each in much the same way and things distinguished must strike us differently; and for that to happen the things in

11

question must actually be, respectively, alike and different. I conclude that the valid part of Dewey's instrumentalist theory that concepts are human constructions is that facts about human beings determine the selection of those features of reality that are conceptually registered but that it is genuine features of reality that the selection is made from.

Dewey's critique of the spectator theory of knowledge does not confine itself to the passively intellectualist account that theory gives of concept-formation. The formation of beliefs, Dewey maintains, as well as that of the material of belief, is a species of human action, not just the passive absorption of what he calls 'antecedent reality'. One slightly puzzling way in which this position is expressed is in the statement that a belief is a 'plan of action'. It is clear enough that beliefs are frequently *parts* of plans of action, in the ordinary sense of the phrase; indeed, it is hard to think of anything that could be called a plan of action that does not at least imply or presuppose some belief or beliefs. But a belief can plainly be held without being part of any actually formulated plan of action in the mind of the believer, such as my belief that Sirius is a very large star.

Dewey generally sees inquiry as the result of some obstacle to action and no doubt it often is. In this situation the inquiry succeeds in removing the obstacle to action by arriving at a belief which makes the formation of an effective plan of action possible. The door is locked and I cannot get in. I look inquiringly for the key under the mat, find it there, and, in a twinkling, I form and put into effect the plan of picking it up, putting it in the keyhole and opening the door.

The process of inquiry that terminates, if successful, in the formation of a belief will typically be itself a form of action. In the minimal case the action is that of just looking attentively. But commonly that is not enough. I see something that looks like a key in the shadows above the lintel. I think to myself 'if that is a key it will feel hard and cool to the touch' and put into operation the verificatory manoeuvre of reaching out to touch it. The confirmation of initially insecure beliefs is an exploratory, experimental process of action, so the belief-forming process of inquiry is itself a kind of action. But it is not, so to speak, all action. The hypothetical statements that set out potential confirmations of what we are inclined to believe suggest experimental lines of action that we can follow. But once the action suggested has been performed we just have to wait and see (or feel) to exercise our negative capabilities of sentience. My reaching out and touching the key is something I do; the hardness and coolness I then feel it to have is something the world (or the key, if that is what it is) does to me.

It is through an extreme of nebulosity at this point in his account of the nature of inquiry that Dewey arrives at his most surprising conclusion: 'inquiry is the controlled or directed transformation', he writes, 'of an indeterminate situation into one that is so determinate in its constituent distinctions and relations as to convert the elements of the original situation into a unified whole'. Or again: 'the outcome of the directed activity [sc. of inquiry] is the construction of a new empirical situation in which objects are differently related to one another and such that the consequences of directed operations form the objects that have the property of being known'.

In any situation of inquiry three sorts of change may be brought about. To start with there is change simply on the side of the inquirer. He was in a state of ignorance ('I don't know where the key is'); he arrives at a state of knowledge or well-founded belief ('Here is the key'). Second, there may be some change introduced by the experimental activity of the inquirer which affects the object of his inquiry. He picks the key-like thing up, has a good look at it, and concludes that it is a key. Here the key is no longer where it was, but in his hand and near his eyes, but it is still a key. Finally, he may bring about a change in the object which, as it were, frustrates the original purpose of the inquiry: 'Where is the key?' 'Well, it's in my hand now.' Or, more catastrophically, 'Where is the egg?' 'It was in my hand but now it's all over the place.'

The third kind of change is not the essence of effective, practical inquiry; it is its nemesis. It is something to be carefully guarded against, not welcomed. 'We murder to dissect' is not a metaphysical truth, but it is a methodological caution.

Beliefs are, then, often for action and they figure essentially in plans of action. In seeking to arrive at well-founded beliefs we commonly engage in experimental activity which is intended to produce a change in us and is ordinarily going to produce some change, even if not a very central or intrinsic one, in the object experimentally acted upon, its relative position, for example, its condition of illumination and so on. But if it centrally alters the object itself the experimental aspect of inquiry defeats its own purpose. At some stage in inquiry the inquirer must be a spectator, however questioning and actively experimental or manipulative he may be at other stages. The object must be left room to do its part. If we put it to the question, it still has to give the answer. Dewey seems to represent the inquirer as a kind of inefficient torturer who does not discover the crucial thing his victim knows but rather what his victim thinks he would like to hear. Dewey is right to stress that inquiry, the acquisition of knowledge or rational belief, is an interaction between the object and its investigator. But it is an interaction, not just the converse of the one-way process presented by the spectator theory of knowledge.

5 Naturalism

Dewey's emphasis on the active nature of inquiry rather strongly implies that the inquirer should be conceived as an intelligent organism, physically interacting with the objects he investigates, and not just as a contemplating mind. It does not strictly entail that conclusion, since a disembodied Cartesian mind could be thought of as being in a way active in his contemplative operations, if only by the directing and focusing of his attention. But Dewey would rightly insist that in fact the confirmation of our beliefs involves bodily manipulation of their objects.

Many philosophers have pointed out the close connection between the spectator theory of knowledge and the tendency of theorists of knowledge to identify perception with sight. In visual perception, for the most part, the action of the body is minimal: sometimes it is just a matter of focusing the eyes; on many occasions no more bodily action is required than moving the head.

But touch, after all, is as important to our perception of the external world as sight. As Warnock has said, although sight is very informative and detailed in its deliverances, we rely on touch in the end for a final check on what sight prompts us to believe.

No one, in fact, would deny that the perceiver is, at least in part, a physical thing causally interacting with the rest of the physical world, or that causal influence exercised on the physical mechanism of perception by its objects is a necessary condition of anything being perceived at all. But what Cartesian theorists of knowledge would maintain is that these propositions, although true, do not affect the epistemology of perception. The knowledge they express, although it is perfectly genuine knowledge, for which any adequate theory of knowledge must find a place, is still knowledge of a secondary, derivative, theoretical kind. They can invoke the same arguments they have used to show that in visual perception all that we really or directly perceive is private entities in our own streams of consciousness to domesticate or subjectivize the deliverances of touch and organic sensation. There are, after all, touch-illusions, such as the effect of rubbing one's hands up and down together with a wire mesh between them, which makes the wire feel like cloth or silk, and once these are admitted there is an entering wedge through which the distinction between the touch-data we directly perceive and the actual tactile properties of things can enter.

In a thorough discussion of these neglected areas of touch and organic sensation H. H. Price interestingly traces the conception of causation as some kind of active efficacy, and not just the kind of regularity which is all that vision finds in it, to the experience of forceful resistance we have, by way of muscular sensation, when objects impinge on us or we press against them. At one point he says that the resistance we experience is essentially relational in nature and so no inference is required to establish an external resistor. But he is equally emphatic that we must not fail to distinguish the sense of embodiment which is the constant background to all our sensory experience from the fact of being embodied which that sense no doubt encourages us to accept as a fact but is not entailed by it.

To insist that we are, as perceivers, embodied organisms in physical interaction with the external world we perceive does not really undermine the sceptically Cartesian account of the indubitable foundations of empirical knowledge. It only highlights in a forceful way the oddity of the Cartesian account of the knower. That oddity is not enough on its own to refute the Cartesian position. After all, the Cartesian is usually going to find a place for these facts in his overall view of the structure of knowledge. To refute his basic subjectivism it is necessary to confront it more directly, as is done by the defence of fallibilism that I expounded earlier. But once we free ourselves of the ultimate Cartesian principle that all our knowledge begins and owes its ultimate confirmation to facts we perceive immediately about the contents of our own minds, the fact that we are, as perceivers, embodied organisms, physically interacting in perception with the world that we perceive, can be placed at the logical and psychological beginnings of our acquisition of knowledge about matters of empirical fact and not be represented, as in Cartesian subjectivism, as a matter of more or less sophisticated and precarious theory.

6   The social nature of knowledge

Every theorist of knowledge would admit that most of what we actually know or rationally believe we owe in some way to others. In recognition of this fact they usually append to their lists of the sources of knowledge some reference to testimony or authority. It will be tacked on in a rather undignified way at the tail end of a sequence that begins with perception and runs through self-consciousness or introspection and memory to inference. Quite often, indeed, testimony is regarded as a special case of inference, deriving its conclusions from premises of the form 'A says p' and 'most of what A says is true'. The first of these is established by perception, the second by induction from observed correspondence between what A has been heard to say in the past and what we have found out to be true on our own.

There is an interesting problem about testimony. Plainly we believe a lot of it when we are not in a position to affirm the generalizations about reliability which would be needed for such beliefs to be rationally accepted. What is more, when we do come to check on the reliability of external informants, we do so with critical instruments with which we have been externally supplied. I have argued elsewhere that this problem can be solved, that the tests we use on testimony are not, as the problem suggests, potentially corrupted at the source. The nerve of the argument is that other people could not mislead us about logic and perception, which are all the testing instruments required. They could perhaps prevent us from learning to speak at all, by energetically random utterance in our presence, but if they are to teach us to speak at all they cannot help teaching us more or less correctly, that is to say in accordance with the rules with which their observable practice has conformed.

Cartesian minds are isolated things, epistemological Adams or Crusoes, making their way in the world on their own. Dewey's intelligent organisms pursue warranted beliefs in a society of other inquirers like themselves and in communication with them. This, once again, is something we all know but it occupies a very small and marginal place in Cartesian theories of knowledge. To draw attention it is not, as it stands, an *argument* against such theories, except to the extent that it brings out the extent to which their assumptions about the foundations of knowledge lead them largely to ignore the actual character of knowledge in a world of social beings. Dewey's pursuit of a theory of knowledge that will be concerned with the actual problems of men here once again opens up a range of problems about knowledge which the tradition to which he is opposed has largely neglected.

2   Language and experience

Jerome Bruner,
Eileen Caudill and Anat Ninio

Let us begin with a Dewey theme. It is that the shape and structure of human experience and human action are reflected in the very nature of language, that language is not itself a system of logic, and that more precisely, the uses to which language is put by any given individual, the linguistic procedures he will employ, necessarily reflect the circumstances in which he has lived and how he has coped with them. In a word, language itself is in some deep sense a record of human experience and its particular personal manifestation is a record of individual experience. In contemporary jargon, language is never to be understood as context independent.

This theme would surely be neither surprising nor particularly timely were it not for two historical circumstances. The first of these is the revolution that has occurred in the study of language over the past two decades – particularly since 1957 when Noam Chomsky's *Syntactic Structures* exploded like a star shell in the world of linguistics. Now, better equipped with data and with manageable doubts, we are able to re-evaluate what that revolution accomplished and what it distorted. Alfred North Whitehead, saluting Lord Russell for a talk he had just given at Harvard on the meaning of quantum theory for the philosophy of science, ended by thanking him for a lucid account that had managed not to obscure the great darkness of his subject. I think we can say of the Chomskyan revolution in linguistics that while it elucidated the nature of syntax, it did in fact obscure the darkness of other, perhaps more important, aspects of language – those precisely that were context dependent. No doubt, by sharply distinguishing the structural from the context-dependent features of language, Chomsky moved formal linguistic theory ahead. My only worry is that that forward movement was dearly paid for by those interested in the acquisition of language, where the separation leads to confusion. But I am

18

not a linguist. My concern over the last several years as a psychologist has been to understand how it is that the child so quickly, and seemingly so easily, learns to use the instrument of language. So swift is the course of that learning that we have been tempted to assume that the child has an innate capacity for language and that this capacity existed in the form of innate ideas about grammar. That conclusion was forced artificially by Chomsky's sharp distinction.

This brings me to my second historical circumstance. It is the new turning point that has been reached in the study of language acquisition, and since history requires an apparatus of dates and places to make it memorable, I shall choose as my *locus* London, the occasion being the Third International Child Language Symposium held in September 1975 at the School of Oriental and African Studies. Two things were evident at that congress. The first was that the doctrine of syntactic primacy in the study of language had died, perhaps of fatigue, and the second was that a new and interesting period had begun in which experience and function had emerged afresh as central to our understanding of what makes it possible for the child to pass so quickly, and so seemingly effortlessly, into the initial use of language. With this new realization, the Dewey theme with which I started this lecture returns to the centre of the stage. I should like to use the occasion of this talk to re-examine it in the light of work now in progress on language acquisition — some of it, indeed, being conducted by my colleagues and myself at Oxford, but much of it scattered from Stanford to Warsaw, from Edinburgh to Jerusalem.

Before I start, first with the demise of syntactic primacy and then with work on language acquisition, let me say a few words about John Dewey's view of language and experience. You will recall the central point in his discussion of the relationship of thinking and experience in his celebrated essay on 'Thinking in education'. He comments: 'No thought, no idea, can possibly be conveyed as an idea from one person to another. . . . The communication may stimulate the other person to realize the question for himself and to think out a like idea. . . . ' In his discussion of this point he makes much of the relationship between experience and thought.

19

Experience for Dewey involved two conjugate components: an active and a passive one, which he characterized by the plain terms *trying* and *undergoing*. Meaning emerges, thought and experience are connected, when trying and undergoing operate jointly — when the former, trying, develops the connections and consequences inherent in undergoing. What makes difficult the *transmission* of ideas by communication, in Dewey's view, is precisely that the process of connection cannot be achieved by the communication itself, but only by the activity of the recipient goaded by the communication, aided of course by the possibility of transaction between members of a dialogue in the interest of 'making ideas clearer'. In fact, Dewey was little concerned with the details of language, and probably his adherence to particular doctrines, like the pragmatic theory of truth, would be found wanting by thoughtful philosophers of language. But what is extraordinarily clear in his writing is a view about language comprehension as an active, constructional process — trying rather than undergoing, in his sense — that may serve us later in examining the state of our knowledge about language and experience.

So let us turn to the doctrine of syntactic primacy in language acquisition, its rise and fall. It begins with Chomsky's efforts to describe formal discovery procedure as one of the goals of linguistics. Such procedures could be seen as mechanisms that take the corpus of a language (or some sample thereof) as input, yielding a grammar as output. The first actual proposal for such a machine was made in a conference paper by Miller and Chomsky in 1957, but that paper was never published and the two authors have since lost the copies they had. So the birth of LAD, like most heroic births, is wrapped in the mystery of the lost child. The idea that such a machine might serve as the basis for initial language acquisition by the child seems not to have occurred to Chomsky until 1960 (see Chomsky, 1962) when he set forth the following proposition at a conference:

We might attempt to construct a device of the kind:
    (1) utterances of L → ☐ → formalized grammar of L.
    This represents a function that maps a set of observed

utterances into the formalized grammar of the language of which they are a sample. Given as input a sufficiently large and representative set of utterances of any language (English, Chinese, or whatever) the device (1) would provide as output a formalized grammar of this language. A description of this device would therefore represent a hypothesis about the innate intellectual equipment that a child brings to bear in language learning.

The device was later to be called the Language Acquisition Device or LAD.

It had several notable properties, and since this account is meant as an obituary rather than an analysis, we shall only single out those that have some relevance to our future consideration of the deceased. For one, it was postulated that mastery of the grammar of a language was independent of mastery or experience outside the domain of language. LAD was thought of as a hypothesis generator, trying out hypotheses based on innate linguistic universals for their fit to the surface structure of the local language. Other forms of experience were irrelevant. A second feature, of course, was that meaning had little or no place in the system of acquisition, nor was language acquisition affected by the extra-linguistic function for which the language was being used. This was consonant with the third feature of the theory: the input corpus of the language was in effect an overheard sample of speech and no specification was made concerning how that input had to be regulated. The learner was, so to speak, an eavesdropper at the adult language feast.

That is sufficient, although it may leave some of you not familiar with the details, rather in a cloud with respect to such terms as linguistic universal, surface structure, and so forth.

The only point I wish to make is that the doctrine of syntactic primacy rested on the idea that language was separate from experience, that its acquisition was based on innate appreciation of structure without regard to meaning and use, and that how the language was encountered did not matter, save that the encounters provide a decent sample of the surface structure of the local language that would allow for

21

recognition of its likeness to linguistic universals. I think I can say, without either the danger of exaggeration or of denigrating the enormous contribution of Chomsky, that each one of these conceptions was deeply, non-trivially mistaken. Language acquisition does depend upon mastery of non-linguistic concepts (although it is not explained by them); the mastery of syntax *is* dependent upon meaning and it may well be better to think of initial syntax as itself serving a semantic function; and finally, the corpus of speech that is the input upon which acquisition is based is not a sample, not overheard, not indifferent. In fact, the corpus of speech to which the child is exposed is governed by rules of interdependent interaction between child and adult and the uses to which language is put are powerfully important in how the child gets into the language. Indeed, in some respects, ironically enough, the adult could be thought of as a kibitzing eavesdropper at the child's linguistic feast. Or better yet, the child and the mother-tutor learn how to use each other as linguistic informants. There may be one additional point worth making, for it relates to the issue of generativeness in language. As Ferrier commented at the International Symposium and as we have also noted, the child is exposed to an extraordinarily limited and repetitive range of learning during the period when he is first getting started on his career as a speaker. The same things are said over and over again in like contexts.

But please note that understanding the world by forming good working concepts of it, depending upon meaning to get the hang of what is being said and how it must be said, and having continual interaction between mother and child as a dialogic carrier-wave for language, still does not account for how the child learns the lexico-grammatical procedures of language, or how he swiftly masters its subtle and systematic phonology; for the procedures of language, while not arbitrary in my view, are not of the same stuff as the concepts by which we organize the world to which language refers and which language is capable of representing. The syntax of a language, the relation of words to each other in utterances, still awaits acquisition: its category rules, privileged orders, its techniques of inflecting, its pre- and post-positioning, its modes, its methods of tense-marking. These are not explained away by saying that LAD is insufficient or even that it is a brave but silly idea, a logician's fantasy. We are now, rather, face to face with the task of trying to understand how the former set of things — the child's knowledge of the world, his knowledge of interaction, and his sense of the extra-linguistic functions that must be served by procedural rules of language — how this knowledge helps him master the latter set of things — the actual procedural rules that make up the linguistic code. Simply because the effort to explain it all by assuming that mastery of syntax is innately determined has failed, does not mean that we have now succeeded by other means. The work still lies ahead, and it is that work to which we must now turn.

I should like to organize the discussion around two general problems. The first has to do with what Michael Halliday calls the mathetic function of language — informing, getting knowledge, using heuristic devices like questions, etc. — and I want to confine myself to that range of events that starts toward the end of the first year with 'pure pointing' and ends with the astonishing process of labelling and primitive predication. When last I spoke at this university, about a year ago delivering the Doris Lee Lecture, I was concerned with the period before that. We go on from there this evening. The second topic is, to use another Hallidayan term, the pragmatic function: how the child uses language 'performatively' (as John Austin would have put it) to negotiate his relations with others — getting them to help him, expressing his affiliation with them, regulating their behaviour.

About the mathetic function, in my previous lecture of last year, I spoke of the manner in which mother and infant came to manage joint reference by procedures for singling out which among a set of alternative events or objects they each had in mind — by monitoring each other's gaze direction, by using distinctive phonological markings, by developing primitive and idiosyncratic labelling procedures, by developing demonstrative heuristics like showing, etc. Most of this activity had the property that what was attended to by the child and what he brought to his mother's attention tended to be in the category of events that might be called 'objects of desire'. Attention, in the main, subserved intended action with respect to objects. The exceptions in large part were certain familiar persons, Mama, Dadda, baby-sitter, etc. They were the recipients of greetings, of inexplicable labelling, etc. So, too, certain familiar objects that achieved special labelling.

With pure pointing, something else enters the scene. *Pure* is used to characterize the kind of pointing that is not an abortive reach toward a desired object. It is a distinctive gesture, involving an extended forefinger, and in the child, Richard, about whom most of my remarks are relevant, it begins at about 12 months — perhaps a little late by the usual norms we find. Before I comment on the contexts in which such pointing first appeared, I should say something about a classic issue in linguistics that I am sure many of you are acquainted with. It is the issue of the familiar versus the unfamiliar, that which is explicitly marked by utterance or gesture or other procedures, and that which remains unstated, presupposed, implicit. We have some indication that before pointing occurred, Richard was already making the distinction by the use of some idiosyncratic vocalizations — greeting familiar situations and objects and pictures with either *geki* or *dede*. It is not the least surprising that he could distinguish the two kinds of situations or that he found ways of indicating that he could — for example, he would look back at his mother when faced with a novel object, not with a familiar one, or smile at familiar situations. What *is* surprising is that he should embody the distinction in a vocal gesture.

The first steady rounds of pointing occurred when Richard went on holiday with his family to the Lake District. His date for videotaping occurred during this absence, so we followed him: his age 14 months 3 weeks. (There had been 6 pure points in a half-hour session when Richard was 13 months 1 week.) The filming was done out of doors, in relaxed rural surroundings, much of it novel to Richard. During the 30 minute period of observation put on tape, there were 35 pure points. In a 3 hour period of baby-sitting plus an hour's walk, more than a hundred episodes of pure pointing were observed, the type of high-frequency occurrence that characterizes new functions early on. All of these were directed to objects that had the following characteristics: (a) if objects were distant more than a metre and therefore out of reach, (b) they were, as objects, in some way unfamiliar or unexpected, (c) they were, if neither an object nor novel, a picture or drawing of a familiar object, or (d) if they were none of these, they were imaginary. By an 'object' is meant person, animal, or thing contained within a small and finite locus. It will immediately be apparent that the rule is one that might be called a distancing principle: pointing occurs when an object is just distant enough, in some dimension, to be interesting and yet not an immediate object of desire to be grasped or pursued or possessed. It may well be that, indeed, some of the objects — cows and sheep — were both interesting and possibly a bit frightening. Let me illustrate with instances of the rules. Distant, unfamiliar objects: sheep, cow, baby in pram, bird, experimenter. Depicted familiar objects: at least six familiar objects in a picture book. Imaginary objects: pointing upward and saying /bə/, the designation also when pointing at birds seen flying above him. Most instances of pointing were accompanied by vocalizations, usually of a non-specific, non-standard type. The example of /bə/ is an exception.

Now, there is one big exception to the rules, and it is an exception produced by the nature of dialogue between mother and child. The mother can be conceived of as having the special role of rendering the novel and the unfamiliar quite banal in response to the child's pointing. The first recorded instance of pure pointing entered in the diary his mother keeps for us (12 months 3 weeks) is directed toward a woman visitor, a stranger to Richard, at some distance from him. This is a sign for the mother to label with the usual, 'Yes, Richard, this is Mrs So-and-so.' This illustrates one of the ways in which pointing is handled: by labelling. The other is by the mother bringing the distant object indicated by the child's 'pure' pointing into the child's reach or possession. At 14 months 3 weeks we have recorded a session in which Richard points to a flower. His mother labels it, picks the flower, and gives it to Richard. He runs his extended forefinger around the edge of the blossoms, silently, and very quickly discards the flower. His attention is not caught by the possibility of manipulation. It would seem that pointing is a technique for marking an object, person, or event, to proclaim its presence to another. When he points to an object, he either then looks at his mother or she is so close by (as in 'book-reading') that her joint line of regard is presupposed. It is of note, too, that he almost always vocalizes in some way. (Another of our children, Jonathan, was observed upon waking and before his parents joined him, to point to a picture on the wall, but without vocalization, the video camera having been set up the night before. But generally, his pointing starting at 10 months was accompanied by /Eh/ when others were present.)

An example of the marking use of pointing for dealing with the novel is provided by Jonathan at 13 months 1 week. We brought a set of new toy animals to a session at his house and placed them on the mantel out of reach. Jonathan entered the room and was immediately caught by them. He immediately pointed to them, swinging his point over the set of three. He did not point to anything else in the room.

Given the interactive nature of language acquisition, it is not surprising that mothers very quickly come to exploit the new skill in pointing. The most outstanding of such is by the incorporation of pointing and accompanying vocalization into rhetoric information exchanges regulated by WH- interrogatives. Indeed, it is the ideal setting for the introduction of the forms of the locative. Typically, the mother will ask the child, 'Where's the ——?' choosing as her referent some changing or otherwise attention-worthy object like a light or aeroplane flying overhead. The child obliges by pointing, initially with an indifferent vocalization — Richard used a variety of these, while Jonathan used either /Eh/ or /m̥/. It is interesting to note that the child obliges by pointing, operating on some sort of Gricean maxim that within limits, such requests should be met. But the style of meeting them indicates that the exchange is understood as rhetorical. The point, in answer to such persistent WH- questioning, becomes perfunctory and may omit altogether both vocalization and looking to the mother.

The child has his ways of exploiting his new skill as well, for he now occasionally incorporates pointing into well-established routines that he enjoys. It happens, for reasons that will be apparent shortly, that we have been studying the development of give-and-take or exchange formats. The reason is rather evident: language is itself an exchange routine and we wish to examine how it is co-ordinated with other such routines. In any case, Richard, shortly after the first appearance of pointing, inserted it into give-and-take games. But the pointing is principally reserved for objects that involve a choice of alternatives or that are ambiguous with respect to choice by being too distant for Richard to take directly. Two examples are interesting. Richard had given his mother two cups. She placed one on her head and the other in her lap, both out of reach. He pointed to the one on her lap and then continued the point to the top of her head, vocalizing. We are not sure if he was demanding. His behaviour did not seem exigent. The other relates to the stabilized struggle over our microphone for the audio-recorder (we use both video and audio, the former being inadequate for phonological analysis). It is a 'forbidden' object. Richard persisted in asking for it when it was lying on the rug within sight. He reached toward the microphone, too distant to reach, pointed at it and vocalized, and looked at the experimenter. Let it be noted, paradoxically enough, that this incorporation into action situations occurs early after the appearance of pointing, is never frequent, and seems to decrease in proportion, as pointing becomes established as a device for rather purer forms of information exchange.

We come now to the stage at which pointing and vocalizing begin to go through a new transformation, concerned now with standard vocal labelling. Here we must begin by picking up a point not developed earlier — the importance of distancing by the use of two-dimensional representation of three-dimensional objects, animals, and persons. I refer of course to the picture book, an enormously useful bit of technology in language acquisition. When books are first introduced, the child typically treats them like other objects — to be banged, carried, mouthed, clawed over. The first task is to get the child to look at the pictures without taking hold of the book as an object — the attentional system and the manipulatory system seem initially to be in conflict. The first point is usually a forefinger dragged across the page on which an object is depicted, usually terminated by a scratching movement. Then there appears a smiling, touching reaction to the picture — either with the palm or the fingers. The child then comes to sit back, looking, with excited vocalization, and with recognition cries for familiar objects. Posture has changed from reaching and grabbing to sitting back. The child now treats the book as a source of information and delight and will fetch his book either spontaneously or in response to a WH- question from mother — like 'Where's Baby Bear?'

Mother uses many attention-getting techniques initially to get the child focused. But soon the child is able to direct attention himself and to point and vocalize at familiar pictures. Notably, the mother's own pointing behaviour becomes concentrated in book-reading sessions. At the same time, she is doing a great deal of labelling of indicated pictures. There is, in the Richard corpus, a tenfold increase in book-picture labelling (in a half hour) between 12 months and 15 months. These labellings are of highly familiar objects, most usually, and there is an enormous amount of revisiting of the same pictures. What can be readily discerned in the growth of book-reading is a distinctive cyclic pattern. The first phase is characterized by the mother asking the child what a given depicted object is: 'What's *that*?' or 'Where's the piggy?' or 'See Jack and Jill.' The emphasis is not upon labelling, but upon getting the child to point discretely to an object labelled by the mother. If we look at Richard in this first phase (about 11 months), we find that his response rate in reaction to different manoeuvres by the mother, where his response is defined as looking, a vocalization, smiling, or touching, is 75 per cent to her labelling, 50 per cent to her 'Look', and none at all to her WH- questions. Any time the child vocalizes during this first phase, she invariably accepts the vocalization as correct, with a 'Yes, that's right; that's a *rabbit*.' She is never corrective in tone or in vocabulary. During this phase, the child readily lapses back into pounding or grabbing the book, etc. In the second phase, once the child has achieved better control of 'inactive attention' and when he is responding steadily to the mother's labelling, the mother's WH- questions (previously not responded to at all) are now the ones most likely to evoke response. Now, 79 per cent of mother's WH-questions are reacted to, and labelling is only responded to 17 per cent of the time, with 'Look' yielding a 47 per cent response rate. His typical response to the WH- question is pointing and vocalizing. There is a stunningly regular pattern that emerges. If the child points and vocalizes, mother will virtually never ask a WH- question in response. She will either give a confirmatory label or an elaboration. If, on the other hand, Richard points and does *not* vocalize, the mother invariably asks a WH- question. What the child is being presented with is an implied demand from the mother to complete a deictic gesture with a label. If the two are not present, she will continue the dialogue until both have occurred. Note that at this stage, the child vocalizes in strings of babbled syllables.

This brings us to the next phase in which, now, the mother starts imposing stricter acceptance limits on the child's response in picture dialogue. She will, once she is sure that the child will vocalize to each exchange, begin imposing the following constraint. Before, if he vocalized, she would never use a WH- question in reply. Now, if the child's vocalization is non-standard or babbled-syllabic, she *will* ask a WH- and even correct his utterance, and not give approval. She may lighten the situation by laughter, but the insistence is there. She is now fishing for phonological hypotheses: the child is expected now to use her vocalization as a model. Of course, given that imitation is in the child's bag of tricks, whatever imitation may be, the child obliges within limits.

In Richard's case, by 15 months labelling is well established. It is interesting to note that his labelling now begins to enter into other contexts in a rather interesting way. Again, give-and-take routines provide an interesting tracer. At 17 months, Richard is very much master of handing off objects, expecting them back, and possibly by now expecting objects in exchange. These exchanges are often marked with vocalizations at the point of intention and of accomplishment (reminiscent of DeLaguna's proclamations of intent and accomplishment), but the vocalizations are babble-like and non-referential. Now, for the first time, he hands an object to a partner — in this case one of the experimenters — and labels the object at the same time. We do not yet know whether it is important to note that the object in this case was a flat plastic lid being used and exchanged as a pretend hat, the vocalization being an ill-formed *hat*. There is also labelling for seeming self-consumption. In the same session, Richard comes unexpectedly upon a biscuit lying on the floor. He stops, takes it to his mouth, and vocalizes *biki* without looking at anybody. Again, it may be an instance of marking the unexpected.

The history of labelling is itself rather intriguing, for what is striking about it is that many nominals during the one-word phase appear and then disappear. Bloom (1973), for example, notes that while her Allison had a cumulated or 'diary' vocabulary at 16 months of some fifty words, there were never more than twenty or twenty-five of them in play during any single week. The others had gone underground, sometimes to reappear in original form, sometimes transformed, as *dog* disappearing and then reappearing months later as *bow-wow*. It may well be that these labels are used initially for utterance as a means of marking. Once the object named falls into its place, becomes part of the context, its label drops out. Greenfield and Smith (1976) notice in a consonant fashion that words are used for those aspects of a situation where there is still some uncertainty. Thus, an object being pursued may be named. Once it is in hand, it is virtually never named. In some deep sense, then, the procedures of language are taking over functions previously fulfilled by other procedures for drawing attention to what is new in contrast to what is presupposed or given. But the step forward is a very genuine one for it permits a generalizability in use that was simply not there before with such primitive devices as pointing, showing, or marking in other ways.

We may return to Dewey's point for a moment. Plainly, the task of language acquisition involving labelling requires a form of interaction that stimulates the child to take on linguistic functions on his own. As Dewey says, communication by itself does not accomplish anything. In so far as the dialogue between mother and infant succeeds in getting the child to fill his role in exchange — through labelling, through responding to WH- questions, etc., etc. — the child is in fact learning not so much a language, as how to proceed in achieving certain ends by the use of language. The input is not a corpus; the output is not a grammar.

We come finally to the pragmatic function, and unfortunately time is insufficient to say much about its development from the point where I left it last spring. In my previous paper, I commented upon the importance of the emergence of *task structures*, often carried out in play, that had three crucial features — division of labour, externality, and constraint. Division of labour is clear enough, and involves role differentiation between two or more partners. Externality implies simply the continued existence of an interaction format that can be resumed, re-enacted, etc. It exists and is, indeed, labelable. Constraint refers to a rule system or a system of informal demands for each to operate in a way expected by the partner in the format. It was proposed earlier that these interaction formats provide the child with working concepts relevant to later grammar like Agent, Action, Object, Recipient of Action, and the like. In a sense, they provide clues for cracking the grammatical procedural code of the language; and they may possibly also provide hints about order rules which determine that initial grammars in all early language patterns studied involve the orders: Agent-Action, Action-Object, Agent-Object, or Agent-Action-Object, and rarely any reversals of these orders.

What we can report about later development of these well-practised patterns is that they continue to provide segmentation points for the occurrence of the child's vocalizations: vocalizations appear most often at the initiating position and at the completion point — as I commented earlier, as intention and accomplishment markers. With time, they begin to appear as well at crucial intervening points, as when the child, looking for an object to hand to mother in an exchange, vocalizes at the point of finding the object, or when the child develops an operator like *up* to characterize the action desired. These action formats seem to provide the coherence in vocalization that early on led linguists like Bloch and DeLaguna to urge that single words were holophrases, sentence words, or *mot phrases*. In no sense can these formats be regarded as 'action grammars', for they do not specify how sentences should be formed. But they provide a steady matrix into which indifferent vocalizations can first be put, and then standard morphemes. Bloom (1973) brings to our attention the fact that when successive one-word utterances appear, each separated by a proper pause, they begin to take on the property of connectedness between successive singlets: *Mummy . . . chair . . . read* as the child goes about the task of getting a book down and recruiting mother into sitting in a chair and reading a book with her.

We can perhaps add to this picture with a brief analysis of negation as it appears in the well-practised routines that join mother and child. One such has to do with going after objects with sensitivity as to parental permission — or, better, parental prohibition — as in approaching a forbidden object and saying *nonono* with a characteristic prosody. There is another format involving putting objects into a container, the objects often being handed to him by his mother or asked for by Richard and handed by her. At 17 months, after the establishment of early prohibitive negation, the form is generalized to the dimension of appropriate-inappropriate. Objects that cannot be fitted into the narrow opening of his favourite videotape box are now commented upon with head-shaking and *no*. An extraordinarily wide category of 'things that go, things that are permitted, things that fit' is being handled by negation — all related to the action structure in which the child is operating.

I would only say one thing in conclusion. The process of acquiring language is very strongly mediated by a push to manage various extra-linguistic functions — regulating joint attention, relating to others, getting certain tasks completed. The child manages these initially by a diversity of communicative procedures. Mastery of each procedure seems to produce a change, even an abandonment of the procedure. There is often — as in Bloom's recent work and in McNeill's discussions — a question as to why the child goes on to more subtle procedures, such as those contained in grammatical discourse. Our evidence would indicate that, among other things, the mother raises the antes, makes her response some-what contingent upon the use of the more powerful methods — as in our examples of pointing being replaced by labelling. But there are undoubtedly, as Bloom and McNeill argue, reasons of economy as well. Better techniques do lead to less ambiguous outcomes. But the outcomes, I think, are not just linguistic, but extra-linguistic, relating to experience, task prosecution, etc. I think Dewey had a point, and I am not saying this out of courtesy to the great man we are celebrating in these lectures. Communication works because it evokes a function to be fulfilled in the child. He may do a certain amount of rather blind imitating, although that is not clear. Mostly what he is doing is entering into joint operations with his mother-tutor and learning to use communication to bring those operations off — with gentle pressure from the speech community. How much of this is innate? I don't know. I suspect a certain amount of it is — like using vocalization so readily, and entering so easily into interaction, etc. But as another great pragmatist, William James, said, the innate occurs only once; after that it becomes subject to the effects of experience.

Note

We are most grateful to Renira Huxley for her helpful comments.

References

Austin, J. L. (1962), *How to Do Things with Words*, Oxford University Press.

Bloch, O. (1921), 'Les premiers stades du language de l'enfant', *J. Psychol. Norm. Pathol.*, 18, pp. 693–712.

Bloom, L. (1973), *One Word at a Time: the Use of Single Word Utterances before Syntax*, The Hague, Mouton.

Bruner, J. S. (1975), 'Early language acquisition: a spiral curriculum', Doris Lee Lecture, University College, London. For an extension of this paper see 'Entry into early language: a spiral curriculum', Charles Gittins Memorial Lecture, University College of Swansea, 13 March 1975.

Chomsky, N. (1957), *Syntactic Structures*, The Hague, Mouton.

Chomsky, N. (1962), 'Explanatory models in linguistics', in E. Nagel,

P. Suppes and A. Tarski (eds), *Logic, Methodology and the Philosophy of Science*, Stanford University Press.

DeLaguna, G. (1927), *Speech: its Function and Development*, New Haven, Connecticut, Yale University Press.

Dewey, J. (1926), 'Thinking in education', in *Democracy and Education*, New York, Macmillan.

Ferrier, L. J. (1975), 'Dependency and appropriateness in early language development', paper presented at the Third International Child Language Symposium, 3—5 September.

Greenfield, P. and Smith, J. H. (1976), *Language beyond Syntax: the Development of Semantic Structure*, New York, Academic Press.

Grice, H. P. (1975), 'Logic and conversation', William James Lectures, Harvard University 1967—8, in P. Cole and J. Morgan (eds), *Syntax and Semantics*, vol. 3 (*Speech Acts*), London and New York, Academic Press.

Halliday, M. A. K. (1975), *Learning How to Mean: Explorations in the Development of Language*, London, Edward Arnold.

McNeill, D. (1974), 'Semiotic extension', paper presented at the Loyola Symposium on Cognition, 30 April, Chicago, Illinois.

Dewey's theory of interest   3
Alan R. White

1

Though one usually associates Dewey's views on *interest* with his educational theories, they seem to have received essentially their full and final shape in his earliest and pre-educational writings on psychology and moral philosophy. Moreover, they both closely resemble those current among his immediate predecessors and contemporaries, such as Herbart, Mill, Stumpf, Stout, James and Titchener (cf. Arnold, 1906) and in some respects anticipate later psychologists, e.g. in their emphasis on interests as motives and on the personality or self as a system of interests (cf. Berlyne, 1949). Yet all these views of interests derive – as I think Dewey saw quite clearly – not from any empirical work in psychology or education, nor from any moral principles, but from philosophical analyses of the notion of interest. What, therefore, I shall try to do is to see how far Dewey's conclusions about the nature of interest are justified. Others, more skilled than I in the appropriate field, have elsewhere described how far his and other current educational views are supported by the facts about interest (e.g. Wilson, 1971).

Dewey and his contemporaries sought a clue to the nature of interest in the three ideas of *attention, feeling* and *object*. Subscribing in his very first book on psychology (1886, pp. 15–17)[1] to the then fashionable triad of the cognitive, the affective and the conative aspects of mind, Dewey regarded consciousness – the presupposed topic of psychology – as involving a knowledge-obtaining activity accompanied by a self-affecting feeling. This activity is attention and this feeling is interest. Later in the same book (pp. 276–8) interest is said to be the connection of both these elements – i.e. the activity of attention and the self-affecting feeling – with the object to which the attention is directed and which arouses the feeling. The combination of these three elements in interest was reiterated five years later in his first book on ethics (1891, p. 305). There, however, he also committed himself to what I shall later argue is an unnecessary piece of metaphysical nonsense. 'Interest,' he said, 'is the union in feeling, through action, of self and an object. An interest in life is had when a man can practically identify himself with some object. . . .' Five years later still, his first venture into educational theory (1896, p. 90) takes the form of an application of his psychological and moral analyses of *interest*. Here reappear the analysis of interest into three elements and the identification of the person who is interested and that in which he is interested; the latter bolstered up by an appeal to two logico-linguistic features of the word expressing the notion of *interest*, whose force I shall discuss later.

I believe that Dewey was basically right — as were also his contemporaries and immediate predecessors — in his analysis of *interest* in terms of a subject interested, an object in which he is interested, a relation of attention between the subject and object and a feeling which the subject has when he gives this attention to this object. Where, as I shall now argue, he, like his contemporaries, goes wrong is at various times, perhaps from excess of zeal, to succumb to the temptation of identifying interest with one or other of its elements to the exclusion of the others. The identification of interest with attention and its identification with feeling are fallacies which Dewey shared with most of his contemporaries. His own peccadilloes consisted in the identification of interest either with the subject of interest, that is, that which has the interest, or with the object of interest, that is, that in which the interest is had, or with something which he pictured as the union of both the subject and the object.

To see this, let us turn to an examination of the notion of *interest* and its elements.

2

Dewey waivered (cf. 1912, p. 472) between saying, in some places (e.g. 1896, p. 76), that interest is the same as attention — an identification which he sometimes (e.g. 1891, p. 305) attributed, quite wrongly, to ordinary use — that it is a necessary condition of attention, so that every instance of attention is due to interest, and that it is a sufficient condition of attention, so that every instance of interest is manifested in attention. At exactly the same time, Stout was arguing that 'we cannot be feeling an interest in an object without attending to it and we cannot be attending to it without feeling some interest in it' (Stout, 1896, pp. 224—5), while a little later McDougall concluded that 'Interest is latent attention, and attention is interest in action' (McDougall, 1923, p. 277).

Clearly this will not do.

First, the notion of interest can be used both dispositionally and episodically, whereas the notion of attention is used only episodically. Interest is something we can either have or take (or show) and 'to be interested' signifies either having or taking (or showing) an interest. To be too interested in the faults of men to see their virtues is to be of a certain disposition, while to be too interested in one's book to hear the doorbell is to undergo a specific experience. While we cannot take (or show) an interest which we do not have, we can have an interest without at a given moment taking (or showing) it. There is no contradiction in saying that I have been for years interested in limericks, though for months I have taken (or shown) no interest in them nor given any of my attention to them. I can be interested in thousands of things, but take (or show) an interest in only a few at a time. Someone may observe me taking (or showing) an interest, but not observe me being interested, in what lies around me. Ceasing to take (or show) an interest is not necessarily losing interest.

Furthermore, one can be dispositionally interested in doing something one is not at the moment doing, but not taking (or showing) an interest in doing what one is not at the moment doing. Only when one is taking (or showing) an interest, therefore, can the object of one's interest necessarily be affecting one.

Now Dewey clearly recognized at different times the dispositional use of the notion of interest, that is, the idea of having an interest which one is not at the moment manifesting, and the episodic use, that is, the idea of taking (or showing) an interest; for, on the one hand, it was a central tenet of his theory that a child is possessed of, indeed, almost constituted of, a set of interests which it is the job of a good teacher to arouse in order to get the child to take an interest in or to pay attention to the required features of the lesson (e.g. 1896 *passim*). Indeed, I shall argue that Dewey so distorted this dispositional use of the notion of interest as to confuse having various interests with being of a certain character of mind. On the other hand, he was always so impressed by the fact that interest is something we can 'take' as to suppose (e.g. 1891, p. 305; 1896, pp. 90, 95; 1913, p. 16) that interests are necessarily active and result in activities, all of which involve paying attention. Because interest is both dispositional and episodic these two views are perfectly compatible, and not unnaturally Dewey was able in practice to emphasize either one or the other. It was only his apparent failure to see that there were two different uses here that led him to assert, on some occasions, that interest is necessarily an activity and on others that it is necessarily a constituent of one's mind like a desire, instinct or feeling.

More important, however, is the fact that attention is differently related to dispositional interests and to episodic interests because attention itself is only episodic. It is something we can only pay or give and not something we can possess without displaying. Attention, unlike interest, cannot be latent and waiting to be aroused. Even the attentive man is necessarily paying attention. Clearly, therefore, to be (dispositionally) interested in something no more implies to be paying attention to it than it implies to be actually taking (or showing) that interest which one has in it. *A fortiori*, interest cannot be identical with attention.

Nor will an identification of interest and attention work even for taking (or showing) interest. Though one who is at this moment taking (or showing) an interest in something must be paying attention to it, he can be paying attention to it without taking (or showing) any interest in it, and, *a fortiori*, without having any interest in it. It is both logically different and socially more flattering to say that you read a colleague's book with deep interest than to say that you read it with close attention. Neither having nor taking (or showing) an interest is something we can decide, resolve, refuse or reasonably order someone to do as we can decide, resolve, refuse or reasonably order someone to pay attention. Being here and now interested or uninterested is something we cannot help. To keep your attention on something, e.g. to keep staring at the man opposite, is to continue doing what you have been doing, but to continue to take an interest in it is to continue this in a certain frame of mind. It is unfair to blame someone for not taking (or showing) any interest in a way that it is not unfair to blame him for lack of attention. Certainly, one may try to take (or show) an interest in something, but this is rather like trying to feel sorry for someone: however hard we try, we may not succeed. This is why we often say to someone that he might at least look interested or pretend to be interested, just as we say that he might look or pretend to feel sorry. People who want to pretend to have an interest which they do not have or to pretend to be taking an interest which they are not taking, pay attention to certain things and try to look interested, just as people who want to pretend to an affection they do not feel ape the behaviour of the affectionate. Contrariwise, to conceal either your interest or the fact that you are taking an interest in something is not to keep any activities hidden in the way that concealing the fact that you are attending is to conceal an activity.

When our attention wanders from our task, we become absent-minded or we forget it; when our interest wanes, we have grown tired of it. Both the man who loses interest and the man who ceases to take (or show) any interest may, but do not necessarily, stop paying attention, though they will no longer pay attention in the same frame of mind. Attention is glued or fastened on something, interest is sustained or retained in it. There can be reasons for paying attention to something other than those given in terms of interest in it or in something else. People can be made to pay attention by threats and warnings or the call of duty. Most commonly, however, it is some feature of the object of our attention which makes us attend to it; what draws my attention to the clock is its suddenly ceasing to tick or its going off with a bang (contrast 1886, p. 127). But whereas both having an interest in something and taking (or showing) an interest in it can, though they need not, explain paying attention to it, paying attention to it cannot explain either having or taking an interest in it. We may attend because we are interested; we are not interested because we attend. To say that we are interested because we are inclined to attend is not to explain our interest but, as we shall see, to explain the meaning of the word 'interest'.

Whenever Dewey had in mind a child's being dispositionally interested in something, he realized clearly that it need not be at that moment paying attention. Indeed, he stressed that it was just such an interest that the teacher had to concentrate on to capture and hold the child's attention. Equally, he realized, that a child's attention could be brought to bear on something without first arousing its interest, either because its attention was caught by one of those features, such as prominent size or loudness, which instinctively and naturally draw human attention (though he often seems to assume that even these are necessarily interesting, e.g. 1886, pp. 121f.; contrast 1896, pp. 129–30) or because its attention was compelled by threats of punishment or enticed by promises of reward (e.g. 1900, pp. 92–3; 1896, pp. 83–9; 1913, pp. 33–4). He even allowed that a child's attention could at any moment be divided between those things that interested it and those that did not, the latter being, he thought, only 'external mechanical attention' (1896, pp. 85–7; 1900, p. 93; 1913, pp. 9–11; 1916, pp. 207–8). Indeed, for Dewey the greatest and most interesting problem in the analysis of interest was the alleged choice between getting attention by arousing interest and getting it by other methods (e.g. 1896, pp. 76f.). The fact that he thought, as we shall see, that the necessity for this choice rested on a misunderstanding of the relation between the subject and the object of interest does not show that he thought that it was impossible to have attention without interest.

Nevertheless, despite these contexts in which his whole problem and argument presupposed the possibility of paying attention to something without taking (or showing) any interest in it, he seems generally to have assumed and frequently committed himself to the mistaken declaration that, for example, 'attention is always realising some interest of the self' (1886, p. 138; cf. 22, 131) and that 'It is psychologically impossible to call forth any activity without some interest' (1913, p. 2; cf. 1886, pp. 18–19; 1916, p. 408). Only attention which was caught and never attention which was given was allowed to be interest free (e.g. 1886, p. 132). The notion of interest was even built into his definition of attention as its basis (1886, p. 133).

If, then, attention is so far from being identical with interest that to be interested in something neither implies nor is implied by paying attention to it nor is taking (or showing) an interest in it implied by, though it does imply, paying attention to it, how, if at all, is interest related to attention? And did Dewey see this?

Several times he refers to a notion which, I think, gives us the desired clue. In 1886 (pp. 121–3), though he does not always distinguish between catching our attention and attracting it, he equates those features which make an object interesting with those 'features which attract the mind' and the interest of an object with its 'attractive power', while in 1913 the 'lack of interest' of a programme of studies is identified with its 'lack of power to hold attention'.

As we have seen, attention can be demanded but interest has to be aroused. 'Conscientious', 'deliberate', 'willing' and 'unwilling', 'half-hearted' and 'reluctant' are appropriate to attention, but not to interest, for the idea of interest contains the idea of attraction. The bored spectator has difficulty in keeping his eyes and his mind on the game, whereas when he is interested his difficulty is to take and keep them off it. The man who loses interest does not necessarily stop paying attention; but he does lose any inclination to pay it. Interest in something is an inclination to give one's attention to it often coupled with a disinclination to pay attention to anything else. When interest passes over into fascination, the inclination to pay attention becomes an inability not to pay it. 'Fascinating' is the superlative of 'attractive'. To be fascinated by a woman is to be unable to take your eyes or your mind off her. The 'club bore', on the other hand, is one who, by his insistence, compels us to attend against our inclination.

3

The second element which occurs in Dewey's and his contemporaries' analysis of interest is *feeling* (cf. Arnold, 1906). By 'feeling' Dewey meant the way in which any conscious creature is affected by that of which it is conscious; so that, in this wide sense of 'feeling', there is an element of feeling in every mental phenomenon, whether it is, for example, belief, knowledge, perception or thought on the one hand, or desire, emotion, sensation or mood on the other. As Dewey put it, consciousness and experience are never 'colourlessly intellectual' (1886, pp. 16, 276, 286). In his very first work (1886) Dewey called this 'feeling' or 'emotional side of consciousness', this 'way in which the self is affected', *interest*. Hence, he thought not of interest as *a* feeling in the sense in which we might say that fear and pity are feelings whereas belief and perception are not, but of the word 'interest' as a synonym of the word 'feeling'. So the third of this book devoted to feelings usually speaks indifferently of 'feelings' and 'interests'. Later, in the same book (1886, pp. 276–7), however, and in his subsequent writings, he distinguished between this 'mental affection' as 'mere' or 'bare' feeling, and reserved 'interest' for the combination of this feeling with an object and an attentive activity. His early identification of interest and feeling, however, persisted so far as to lead him throughout his life to think of most object-directed feelings as interests. He continued to subscribe to his early view that 'every object that comes within our experience gets some emotional colouring, as it helps or hinders that experience. It thus gains a special and unique interest of its own' (1886, p. 286). So he speaks (1886, pp. 277f.) indifferently of personal, intellectual or aesthetic feelings and personal, intellectual or aesthetic interests (1886, chs XIV–XVI). He equates (1886, p. 340; 1891, p. 305) 'love' with 'interest in a person' and characterizes fear and dislike as the 'obverse aspect of interest' (1900, pp. 44–5). He also assimilates interest and desire, either holding that interest is the same state of mind as desire, but with possession of its object (1891, p. 305; 1886, p. 361), or holding that desire is 'properly mediated interest' (1896, p. 109). For him, being desirable is being interesting (1886, ch. XVIII), a conflict of interests is a conflict of desires (1916, pp. 208–9) and the relation of interest to effort is that of desire to effort (1912, p. 473). To relate one's teaching material to the interests of the child is, for Dewey, to relate it to his 'urgencies and needs' (1900, p. 23).

Now, whether or not Dewey is correct in supposing that everything of which one is in any way conscious necessarily affects one and, therefore, gives rise to what he calls a 'feeling', it is quite clear that, in the first place, being conscious of something no more implies taking an interest in it than, as we saw, does paying attention to it imply taking an interest in it. Second, and more relevantly for our purpose, though interest is certainly something we can, though not necessarily something we must always, feel, it is not in every sense of 'feeling' that we 'feel' interested in things.

'Feeling' interested is obviously not a perceptual feeling like feeling a hole in my pocket, or an exploratory feeling like feeling for a light switch. Neither is someone who is interested in what he is doing necessarily having any sensations, faint or acute, steady or intermittent, localizable or general; such sensations would distract him from the object of his interest. An itching in his fingers might be a sign of interest, it is not the feeling of interest itself.

Moods such as happiness, depression, frivolity, sentimentality, are commonly called feelings. But interest is not a mood, for, unlike a mood, it has, as Dewey stressed, a definite object; nor does it colour one's actions and feelings as a mood does. An apparent objection to this denial that feeling interested is feeling or being in a certain mood springs from the fact that we can certainly call feeling, or being, bored 'being in a certain mood' and also say that 'feeling bored by' something is the contrary, though not the contradictory, of 'feeling interested in' it. The answer to this objection is that 'bored' is used to cover both the mood which consists in a general ability to feel interested in anything and the specific inability to feel interested in a given topic.

Nor is feeling interested an emotion or stirred-up state like feeling excited or thrilled, agitated or surprised. You cannot be 'beside yourself' or 'speechless' with interest; nor does increasing interest disturb your concentration as mounting excitement or anxiety may.

What one feels when one feels interested in anything is, I think, an *inclination* to attend to it. It is what Baldwin long ago called an 'impulse to attend' and Stumpf a 'Lust am Bemerken'. To feel interested in something to which, for whatever reason, one does not or cannot pay attention is to feel an inclination to which one does not or cannot yield. The difference between the man who feels an interest in what he is giving his attention to and the man who does not is that the former is, while the latter is not, giving an attention which he feels inclined to give.

4

For Dewey the ubiquity of interest is due to its invariable presence not only and not mainly as the resultant way in which, that is, the feeling with which, one is affected whenever one is conscious of anything, but also as a motive for every action. Immediately after declaring that 'every object that comes within our experience gets some emotional colouring . . . a special and unique interest . . .', he adds 'an object, as soon as it has become interesting, becomes *an end of action in itself*' (1886, p. 286; cf. pp. 317, 340). The role of interest as a motive is for Dewey much more important than its role as the feeling that accompanies consciousness. He emphasized (1896, p. 120) this as the main difference between his psychology and that of Herbart whose views on interest he otherwise finds very appealing. It is, moreover, the leading role which has been assigned to interest in more recent psychology (cf. Berlyne, 1949). 'Every impulse and habit,' says Dewey, 'that generates a purpose having sufficient force to move a person to strive for its realisation, becomes an interest' (1913, p. 90; 1896, p. 112; 1916, pp. 152–3). Indeed, just as he tended to move from the view that interest is a feeling to the view that the word 'interest' is a synonym for the word 'feeling', so he tends to move from the view that every motive is an interest to the view that the word 'interest' is a synonym for the word 'motive'. Thus, 'motive' is sometimes (e.g. 1908, pp. 321–2; 1896, p. 112) defined as 'those

interests which form the core of the self and supply the principles by which conduct is to be understood'; 'motive' and
'interest' are used interchangeably (1908, p. 322) and 'the
motive force of an end' is declared (1913, p. 60) to be an
equivalent expression to 'the interest that the end possesses'.
Lists of motives are called lists of interests (1913, p. 62), his
doctrine of the identity of self and object is said to be the
key to understanding the nature of both motives and
interests (1908, p. 319), both 'motive' and 'interest' are said
(1908, p. 322) to be applicable either to the desire of an object or to the object desired, e.g. the desire for money and the
money itself, and his dictionary article on 'Interest' opens
with the declaration that: 'The "doctrine of interest" in education is a sort of shorthand expression for a number of different motives' (1912, p. 472).

Certainly, an interest in something like stamp-collecting
provides a possible motive for action; but Dewey's equation
of interests with motives cannot be right, both because someone can have a motive for doing something which is not an
interest in it and can have an interest in doing something
which is not his motive for doing it. Thus, to categorize
jealousy, greed, revenge, love, hatred, ambition or patriotism
merely as interests is to take far too anaemic a view of human
passions. On the other hand, someone's interest in, for
example, stamp-collecting or philosophy need not on a particular occasion be his motive for, for example, buying stamps
or reading a philosophy book; perhaps he was buying the
stamps or reading the book for a friend. Dewey himself on
occasion allowed that motives could be supplied by such
things as needs, cravings and demands (e.g. 1900, p. 40).
Even less correct is Dewey's suggestion that the terms
'interest' and 'motive' are synonymous. Interests, but not
motives, can be aroused, excited or awakened; they can sub-
side, vanish, or be lost; they can devour and consume. Motives,
but not interests, can be plausible or far-fetched, ulterior or
involved. An interest is one of the things that can be a motive,
just as a car can be a gift or a house an asset, but interests and
motives are no more of the same category of things than cars
and gifts or houses and assets.

What I think may have misled Dewey into his identification

of interests and motives or even into his view that interests always motivate are, first, his equation of interest and desire, second, his assimilation of the dispositional use and the episodic use of 'interest' and, third, his failure to distinguish 'doing something from (or for) interest' — which was his main topic — from 'doing something with interest'.

First, though Dewey usually directly equated motives with interests, he also equated motives with desires (e.g. 1886, pp. 366–8; 1900, p. 79) and, as we saw, desires with interests, and, therefore, indirectly motives with interests. But the equation of interest and desire is no more correct than that of interest and motive. Though someone who feels interested in something may not merely feel inclined to give it his attention but also feel a desire to do so, it does not follow, and is not true, that an interest is a desire for anything more than to give one's attention to it. It would be too strong to say that a story which had aroused my interest had aroused my desire and too weak to say that a desire for survival is just an interest in it.

Turning, second, to the way in which an interest undoubtedly can explain what one does, we must remember the distinction between (dispositionally) having an interest and (episodically) taking (or showing) an interest.

Taking (or showing) an interest in, and hence paying attention to, something on a particular occasion may be due to and explicable by the interest that one has long had in it or in this sort of thing. Having an interest, as we saw, is being disposed to take (or show) an interest and, hence, to pay attention. In such an example we are explaining a particular manifestation of a disposition by the disposition itself; we are saying that someone did X on this occasion because he is disposed to do X.

Interest, in this dispositional use, can provide a reason for engaging in any activity and, therefore, for paying attention. Indeed, the sorts of activities which can be said to be done 'from interest' must be such as involve paying attention. Like desire, the sorts of reason that interest thus provides for doing something are twofold. You may do X or X-like things because you are interested in X or because you are interested in Y. In the former case you would say you had done X 'just from interest'. For example, an interest in archaeology may be the reason why someone pays attention to archaeological matters by reading books, attending lectures and joining in conversations on the subject. The sort of reason that interest provides for paying attention to something or for engaging in any activity is similar to that which jealousy provides for certain kinds of behaviour or that brittleness provides for breakages. When you wish to attract someone's attention you try to provide the sort of thing which is liable to do this, something in which he is interested, just as when you want a big smash you get something liable to break, something brittle. Advertisers' hoardings show pictures of pretty girls because, as a matter of definition, 'sex-interested' males will look at them. We are familiar with the anecdotes of psychology textbooks (cf. Dewey, 1886, p. 135) whose point is that people of different interests, when placed in the same situation, pay attention to and notice different features. On their communal walk the geologist notices the rock formation, the botanist the plant life, the painter the landscape, while the philosopher fails to notice anything. But the point illustrated is not, as psychologists sometimes suppose, a factual discovery about human behaviour, not something for which we need experimental evidence; it is a logical truth about the relation of the notions of attention and notice to that of interest.

We can be interested not only in objects and activities, but also in becoming or being or attaining or bringing about something. Ends as well as deeds can attract us. Thus an interest in X can provide a reason for doing Y. The student who is interested in improving his French has a reason for visiting France, buying French newspapers, seeing French films. We often attend to something for its own sake, because we are interested in it, but our reason for attending can also be that we are interested in finding out or discovering so and so. 'Curiosity' is this sort of interest. In these cases of doing X from interest in Y we do not describe ourselves simply as doing X 'out of (from, for) interest'.

Although Dewey did not go so far as to make the mistake of saying that when we do X out of interest in Y, for example because X is seen as a means to Y, we, therefore, do X itself out of interest, he does seem sometimes to have

47

supposed (e.g. 1896, pp. 100–1; 1913, pp. 25–7) that X it-self necessarily becomes interesting to us; indeed, that the interest which originally attached only to the end now attaches also to the means. It is in this way, he thought (e.g. 1896, p. 97; 1900, pp. 43–6, 92–3; 1912, p. 474; 1916, p. 149), that the successful teacher makes things interesting for the pupil and not by any merely external sugar-coating of the pill. 'To make it interesting by leading one to realise the con-nection that exists is simply good sense; to make it interest-ing by extraneous and artificial inducements deserves all the bad names which have been applied to the doctrine of interest in education' (1916, p. 150). So convinced was Dewey that whatever was seen as a means to something in which one was interested — or indeed something which was in any way desired — was, therefore, itself interesting that he several times even used the etymology of 'interest' from 'interesse' (to be between) to prove his point. 'To be "between" the agent and his end,' he said (1916, pp. 149–50; 1896, p. 99), 'and to be of interest, are different names for the same thing.'

Certainly, things, previously indifferent, can and do become interesting when their connection with something in itself interesting is seen (e.g. 1896, p. 100; 1900, pp. 84–7; 1912, pp. 473–4; 1913, pp. 22, 38–41). But this is not necessary. To take Dewey's own example (e.g. 1896, p. 100), surely the fact that a man with a family to support 'has a new motive for his daily work' does not entail that he finds that work any less of a drudgery. Students whose interest in foreign literature leads them to learn the irregular verbs of its language do not necessarily find this learning interesting. An interest in X can make us pay attention to Y without making us take an interest in Y. Dewey, I suspect, was here guilty of the logical error of supposing that if one is interested in, for example, providing for one's family, and providing for one's family takes the form, on some occasion, of disagreeable drudgery, therefore one must, on that occasion, be interested in dis-agreeable drudgery.

When what we do, including the paying of attention to something, is explained not by a continuing interest we have but by an interest we are here and now taking (or showing) or feeling, our explanation is of a different kind. For, since to feel interested is to feel inclined to pay attention, then to pay attention to something because we feel interested in it is to do what we feel inclined to do; our attention satisfies our desire to pay attention. It is when the play is dull that, as Aristotle remarked (*Nicomachean Ethics*, X 5), we turn to our box of chocolates.

It follows from this relation of *interest* and *attention* that the statement 'He was interested in so and so' is what Ryle has called a 'mongrel-categorical' relative to the statement 'He paid attention to so and so'. A reporter might say of a distinguished visitor at an exhibition either that 'He paid particular attention to the toy stand' or that 'He took (or showed) a particular interest in the toy stand'. The description in terms of interest gives an explanatory-cum-predictive account of the same event as the description in terms of attention. It can, therefore, replace it as a description, serve as an answer to the question why he paid attention, and allow us conditionally to predict a continued attention to the toy stand or things related to toys. Further, one can look or listen, examine or study, read or discuss, with attention or with interest.

The third oversight which may have led to Dewey's identification of interest and motive is that between 'doing something from (for, out of) interest' and 'doing something with interest'. Whereas 'from interest' gives the reason for someone's doing something, 'with interest' states the accompanying result of his doing it. Hence 'purely', 'solely', 'merely' — which are used to emphasize the uniqueness of a reason — can accompany 'from interest' but not 'with interest', while 'little', 'much', 'sharp', 'increasing' — which characterize the degree of anything — may accompany 'with interest' but not 'from interest'. Similarly, a non-continuous action, such as asking a question, coming to a meeting, going to Greece, can only be done 'from' and not 'with' interest; whereas a result, like seeing or hearing, coming across or learning something, may be 'with' but not 'from' interest.

A person who reads a book 'from' or 'for' interest shows his interest by doing what he does. His interest explains his reading of the book and allows us to make conditional predictions about the doings of other things of the same sort. No such explanatory-cum-predicative account is given of the reading of a man who is described as 'reading *with* interest'. Nor does 'because he is interested in what he is doing' explain why someone does what he is doing, however well it may explain why he does not do something other than what he is doing or why he continues to do what he is doing or why he pays attention to what he is doing. My interest in the philosophy book I am reading may explain my not giving it up or my not answering the telephone or my attention to my reading. My interest in the book does not, however, explain my reading the book, though my interest in philosophy may.

5

Dewey's theory of interest was, for the most part, that common in the philosophy and psychology of his day. There is, however, one major detail which seems to have been peculiarly his own and which I have with deliberate abusiveness called 'metaphysical nonsense'. It is his identification of the person interested with that in which he is interested or, as he sometimes puts it, the union of self and object (e.g. 1896, pp. 83f.; 1908, p. 321; 1912, p. 472; 1913, pp. 14, 90, 95; 1916, pp. 161–2). He appealed (e.g. 1896, pp. 83f.; 1913, pp. 6–7) to this identity to suggest that both those who advocated discipline, effort and threats and those who advocated blandishments, bribes, and allurements to attract a pupil's attention make a common mis-assumption that the pupil and what he is interested in are two separate things which need to be brought together by some means or other. A similar common mis-assumption with a similar solution underlies, he thought, both the ethical conflict between the utilitarian emphasis on consequences and the opposing emphasis on the moral agent (e.g. 1908, pp. 315–19) and the traditional view that if someone always acts from some interest, he therefore, always acts from self-interest (1908, p. 328).

But what on earth can Dewey have meant by saying that a person − or, as he more usually says, a person's 'self', or 'mind' − who is interested in something is either identical with or forms a union with that in which he is interested? We can, I think, find at least four logico-linguistic features which help to explain what he meant by this and why he believed it to be so.

First, he regarded interest as a feeling which was integrated with the object that aroused it, partly, I suspect, for the sort of reason that led Aristotle to identify pleasure in an activity with the completion of the activity in which one takes the pleasure (cf. 1896, pp. 87–9; 1913, p. 12) and partly because he was struck by the fact that we use the word 'interest', as we use 'pleasure', 'need', 'want', etc., both for someone's interest, pleasure, need, want, etc., and for the object of his interest, pleasure, need, want, etc. Thus, philosophy and stamp-collecting are the interests of the man who is interested in philosophy and stamp-collecting as the sights, sounds and tastes from which we get pleasure are called 'pleasant' (cf. 1886, pp. 276, 289; 1891, p. 305; 1896, p. 91; 1908, pp. 321–3; 1912, p. 475; 1913, p. 16; 1916, p. 148). Similarly, the value of an object is, Dewey considered, our valuation of it (1886, pp. 276, 289; 1896, pp. 94–5). Beauty is both in the eye of the beholder and in the object beholden (1886, p. 322). In short, what is interesting, like what is pleasant, attractive, amusing, desirable, or what is a need or want, is what people find interesting, pleasant, attractive, amusing, desirable, or what they need or want. Now, emphasis on the fact that what one has an interest in is called one's interest could tempt one to single out the object of interest from the three elements of interest — attention, feeling and object — and plausibly — though, of course, quite incorrectly — identify interest with that element. And Dewey does sometimes succumb to this temptation. But clearly none of this would go any way to show that either the interested person or the interest he has is joined with, much less that it is identical with, the object of his interest any more than the analogous feature of pleasure, need, want, etc., shows an analogous union. It would be absurd to say that I am identical with Plato, his dialogues, or his Theory of Forms just because I have an interest in all of these. And it would be equally absurd to conclude from this that since I am identical with each of my interests, then all of my interests are identical with each other.

Second, Dewey appealed to the etymological derivation

of 'interest' from the Latin *'interesse'*, meaning 'to be between', to argue that interest was a bond which annihilated the distance between the interested person and the object of his interest (1896, p. 91; 1912, p. 472; 1913, p. 17; 1916, p. 149). But even if interest did join the two, it would not make them identical.

Third, Dewey seems to have taken too literally various metaphorical expressions of the way in which our interests occupy our mind. Thus, the interested person is said to be 'engaged' or 'occupied', 'taken up with', 'concerned in', 'absorbed by', 'carried away by' his material (e.g. 1896, pp. 83f., 91; 1913, pp. 17, 65, 90; 1916, p. 148); he 'finds himself at home' in it (1912, p. 472). From this, Dewey concludes that what he calls 'completeness of interest' is 'wholehearted identification with what one is doing' (1913, p. 80). But clearly to take these metaphors of absorbed attention literally as identification of someone with what he is interested in is as if a philosopher were to argue that because a colleague on Senate was, as we say, 'at one with him' about a certain measure, therefore he was identical with this colleague.

Dewey's final type of argument for the identification of the interested person and the object of his interest also stems partly from taking metaphors literally. On several occasions an explicit reason for the 'identification of the self with some object or idea' is 'the necessity of that object or idea for the maintenance of self expression' (1896, p. 89; 1913, p. 14). This is rather like identifying oneself with one's needs on the strength of the figurative phrase 'I need it to be myself.' Related to this is the argument that because a man who is interested in his work is said to 'find himself in' the work, whereas a man with a different set of interests would be a different kind of man, a man is, therefore, his interests (1916, p. 408, cf. p. 162; 1913, p. 43). His interests form his core (1908, p. 321); for *interest* defines the self' (1908, p. 327; 1916, p. 408). Dewey held that, 'if we are psychically awake at all, we are always interested in one direction rather than another' (1896, p. 93; 1908, p. 320; cf. 1910, pp. 36f. on 'curiosity'). And he, rightly, argued (1908, p. 322) that, for example, 'hunger', 'benevolence', 'cruelty', and 'kindness', are not the names of entities which make us do things but of tendencies we have to do them. But, clearly, to identify either someone or, more plausibly, his personality, character or mind, with his interest, as we might reasonably, in Aristotelian or Rylean fashion, identify his mind with a set of intellectual and moral abilities, capacities, dispositions and functions, somewhat as we identify a house with the bricks which compose it (1908, p. 316), is to identify his personality with the interests which he has in things and not with the things in which he has these interests, with his inclination to pay attention and not with that to which he pays attention. Here Dewey's argument points rather to the (mistaken) identification of interest with the subject of interest than to the (mistaken) identification of the subject and the object of interest. Only a failure to remember the distinction between my interest in birds' eggs and the birds' eggs which are my interest could lead to the preposterous conclusion that I am somehow to be identified with a collection of birds' eggs.

It is the philosophical absurdity of these four logico-linguistic arguments for Dewey's oft-repeated identification of the subject and the object of interest that makes me dub the identification a piece of 'metaphysical nonsense' and makes me reject it as an attempt to solve the dispute — which Dewey over-exaggerated — between those who look for an incentive to attention in discipline and those who look for it in interest.

6

Finally, just as Dewey was deflected by his digression into metaphysics from any serious attempt to tackle this dispute, so his failure to examine deeply enough the relation between one's interest in something and something's being in one's interest deflected him from any serious attempt to face the possibility of a conflict between them as rival criteria of the purpose of education. He seems to have assimilated (e.g. 1916, pp. 148, 401) the idea of some things being in someone's interests to the idea of someone's being interested in that thing. Hence, to act in one's own interests or in the interests of others was to act with an interest in one's self or with an interest in others and the possibility of conflict between self-interest and the interest of others was treated as a conflict, not between what is in one's own interests and what is in another's interests, but between one's being interested in one's self and one's being interested in others (e.g. 1891, pp. 306—7; 1913, p. 88; 1916, pp. 148, 408). This assimilation was, perhaps, largely due to Dewey's assumption that to be interested in someone entailed being interested in securing what was in his interests (e.g. 1891, pp. 306—7; 1908, p. 326).

But what is in a child's interests may not be what the child is interested in. Indeed, he may have no idea whether something is in his interests or not, but he is hardly likely to be so ignorant of what he is interested in. Things can be done, as Dewey himself writes, in the interests of efficiency, fair play or justice (1908, pp. 330, 344), but such inanimate things cannot be interested in anything. Hence, even if we make the child's interests the corner stone of our educational philosophy, we are still left with the question: 'Should we do what the child is interested in or what is in his interests?'

Note

1 Dates given for Dewey are those of first publication; page references are to editions cited in the References.

References

Arnold, F. (1906), 'The psychology of interest', *Psychological Review*, vol. XIII, pp. 221—38, 291—315.

Berlyne, D. E. (1949), ' "Interest" as a psychological concept', *British Journal of Psychology*, vol. XXXIX, pp. 184—94.

Dewey, J. (1886), *Psychology*; pagination of 3rd edn, New York, 1894.

Dewey, J. (1891), *Outline of a Critical Theory of Ethics*, pp. 304—11; pagination of *The Early Works of John Dewey 1882—1898*, London, 1969.

Dewey, J. (1896), 'Interest as related to the training of the will'; pagination of *Educational Essays*, ed. J. J. Findlay, London, 1910.

Dewey, J. (1900), *The Elementary School Record*, Nos. 4, 5, 6; pagination of *The School and the Child*, ed. J. J. Findlay, London, 1907.

Dewey, J. (1908), *Ethics*, ch. XV; pagination of 1932 edn, New York, 1959.

Dewey, J. (1910), *How We Think*, chs III (section 1), XIV—XV; pagination of 2nd edn, Boston, 1933.

Dewey, J. (1912), 'Interest', in *A Cyclopaedia of Education*, ed. P. Monroe, vol. III, pp. 472—5.

Dewey, J. (1913), *Interest and Effort in Education*, Boston.

Dewey, J. (1916), *Democracy and Education*, chs X, XXVI (section 2), New York, 1960.

McDougall, W. (1923), *An Outline of Psychology*, London.

Stout, G. F. (1896), *Analytical Psychology* (2 vols), vol. 1, London.

Wilson, P. S. (1971), *Interest and Discipline in Education*, London.

4   The self in action
Martin Hollis

Students of human nature used to scour the wide world for
their data. In these more advanced days, however, they may
prefer to consult the *International Encyclopedia of the Social
Sciences*. If so, they will be disappointed. There is no entry
for Human Nature. But then the unity of the *International
Encyclopedia* is that of a shopping centre which just offers a
roof to cognate specialists. In some ways it is a poor replace-
ment for the general store, supplying articles which everyone
needed whatever his special concerns. Those who take the
hint and try the older *Encyclopedia of the Social Sciences*
will indeed find an entry for Human Nature. It is by John
Dewey and is as clear, concise and wide-ranging as one could
wish. Yet it contains a remark at odds with much of Dewey's
own work. 'It cannot be doubted', he writes, 'that there are
some limits to the modifiability of human nature and to institutional change, but these have to be arrived at by experimental observation.' His point seems almost banal. It is that
men are not wholly plastic and that social processes neither
shape nor explain them *in toto*. Yet it springs a twofold sur-
prise, for, in the first place, Dewey must have devoted a mil-
lion words in a long life to casting doubt on the fixity of
human nature and, in the second, was always too much of a
philosopher to leave the truth to experimental observation. I
shall invoke his aid in seeing both what the truth about
human mutability may be and what sort of truth it is. The
question concerns the role of the self in the philosophy of
human action and Dewey's answer will show us the strength
and the snags of a powerful pragmatism.

My reason for turning to Dewey is not just that he is a
noble, systematic thinker, full of perennial insights, wise,
shrewd and blessed with a power of vivid prose.[1] Nor is it
directly the importance of his instrumentalism nor the influence of his views on education. The reason has to do with

56

his way of fusing philosophy and social theory. He is the owner of an up-to-date general store, a modern social philosopher of an old-fashioned sort. I do not mean that his goods are old-fashioned. Indeed, he purveys a solvent for the very latest riddle in action theory, as we shall see. I mean that, like many traditional political theorists, he hopes that the study of men as they are will yield a science of laws as they should be. Accordingly, our theme will be his account of human nature, social action and freedom. Having begun with a gesture to Hegel and a contrast between Humeans and pragmatists, I shall introduce William James's search for 'a basic principle of personal unity' and Dewey's offer to find it in the idea that 'man is a creature of habit'. A theory of freedom follows and its modern interest will be shown by considering Dewey's two notions of motive, which yield a normative theory of the self-in-action to occupy the rest of the paper. Interestingly, it is a theory of self-in-action without a self and there will be complaints from philosophers and sociologists. Yet neither party is in a position to cast the first stone and perhaps neither needs a self, if they will only co-operate. I shall indeed urge them to co-operate under Dewey's guidance, in hope of a new notion of identity and a rational social policy. But they will still need more of a self than Dewey provides, if freedom is, as Dewey has it, a matter of forming institutions to let men translate into social action their essential human nature.

In the *Festschrift* for Dewey's eightieth birthday Gordon Allport complains in a perceptive essay that Dewey can offer no proper theory of personality and Dewey, replying at the end of the volume, more or less agrees.[2] In the end, as I shall try to show, he must. Yet he need not concede easily, since his theory of habit will do almost all he asks of it. 'Man' he maintained, 'is a creature of habit, not of reason nor yet of instinct.'[3] It is a deceptively simple basis but it supports an entire analysis of the self, of social institutions and of human freedom.

We shall do well to remember that Dewey had a Hegelian upbringing. He never threw it off and it remains a distinctive thread in an American pragmatist who saw himself as a good empiricist. But it was not a handicap of the sort which afflicts the socialist born a viscount or the Jew once a gentile, for it gave him a sense that objects are always in a state of becoming, a sense which is the stuff of pragmatism. Admittedly he abandoned his early efforts to psychologize in a Hegelian mode. His *Psychology* of 1886, for instance, employed a self, described as a 'real unity', to account for the connectedness and peculiarity of human experience. It was marked by an idealist belief in the dynamic union, indeed total integration, of experience and nature. Later works, by contrast, treat integration as a rare and precarious construct. Experience is no longer taken as essentially cognitive; feelings and activities are deemed at least as important. Nature ceases to be a single cosmos and its purposive elements shrink to the organic subjects of human sciences like biology. The self drops out of obvious sight, along with its props of will and cosmic impulse. Hegel had yielded to a twentieth-century, matter-of-fact view of man and nature — witness Dewey's wry remark in 1910 that he knew of a college so backward that it was still using his *Psychology* as a textbook.

The Dewey we recognize is a twentieth-century figure who sees no single or rational system in the world and who makes human freedom a fragile creature of education. But Hegel has something to offer a pragmatist, and Dewey in any case was never a high and mighty Hegelian on first name terms with the Absolute. Even in *Psychology* his accent is on process or becoming and the sentence referring to the self as a real unity reads in full: 'The self is a connecting, relating activity and hence a real unity, one which unites into whole all the various elements and members of our knowledge' (part I, chapter 9, section II). This bullfrog of a self asserts more than it explains and Dewey grew dissatisfied with it for that reason. But, although he dropped it from obvious sight, the problem it pointed to continued to vex him and should, I dare say, vex recent pragmatists too.

The problem is one of personal and social identity. It confronts Dewey through his endeavour to work an instrumental theory of knowledge, a view of reality as process and an account of the mind as connected activity into an empiricism descended from Hume. For Hume, experience is given, the knowing mind is passive and there are no links in nature.

Knowledge of the world is therefore referred to perception and habits of association in the mind. Even the relation of cause and effect, which is proclaimed as our sole way of going beyond mere ideas and the data of the senses, reduces, from the standpoint of knowledge, to concomitance. Admittedly Hume allows us imagination and assigns it some role in forming our beliefs. But there is no rational warrant for the work of imagination and it has no place in justifying claims to knowledge. Equally the self, whose ancestor is visibly Descartes's *ego*, turns out to be a mere bundle of passive perceptions. Hume had hoped for a science of man and society from these minimal ingredients but, as he confessed so gracefully in the appendix to the *Treatise*, they did not give him enough. He could not finally explain the principles which unite our successive perceptions in our thought or consciousness. The identity of the self could be neither explained nor explained away.

The last paragraph may be unfair to Hume but it makes a pragmatist line easy to spot. We start by making the mind active instead of passive and make knowledge of the world a matter of construction instead of perception. The mind's job is not to attend to experience in order to discern patterns but to work patterns into experience with the aid of imagination. There are no brute, atomic, uninterpreted facts; judgment, the applying of concepts to experience, occurs a stage earlier than empiricists have been wont to believe. Judgment occurs at the moment of presentation, with the result that nothing is given and the old strategy of erecting a temple of knowledge on certain foundations is to be rejected. Instead of a temple we have a web of beliefs, spun and adjusted by the active mind. The web constitutes knowledge because, I suppose, it satisfies us, perhaps for some reason of principle like economy or usefulness, perhaps because of our human constitution. The theory of knowledge is fused with the philosophy of science to yield a philosophy akin to instrumentalism – or, if it does not, Dewey will be entitled to complain.

In switching from a passive to an active mind, pragmatism sets itself a hard question about how to relate experience, regarded as an interpretation, to experience regarded as a test for beliefs. The latter seems to require givens which the former seems to deny. This is an old problem which remains a centre of dispute. But there is an aspect of the dispute which, from oversight or embarrassment, has been less prominent of late. Even if a passive mind can be passed off as a bundle of perceptions, an active mind is pivotal. In conceiving of knowledge as a web which is woven and rewoven, pragmatism does indeed pose queries about the criteria of design and adjustment. But it poses no less obvious or urgent queries about the weavers. James, Dewey and Mead were brave enough to tackle the topic but they hardly disposed of it. If knowledge and society are to be seen as processes, what shall we say of the spiders in the web, the spinners of the fabric, in a word of the self?

Although we are addressing ourselves to Dewey, we shall, like him, need to lean on William James. Dewey acknowledged his debt to James's justly famous views and dissented from them only enough to make life easy for the social theory of G. H. Mead. James had distinguished between the I and the Me, dividing the latter or phenomenal self into the bodily me, the social me and the spiritual me.[4] His account of the Me is riveting enough but we must restrict ourselves here to the I. Many a pragmatist would brush the I aside but James, bless him, did not. Admittedly he had no patience with substance theories, since 'to say that phenomena inhere in a Substance is only to record one's protest against the notion that the bare existence of the phenomena is the total truth' (p. 346). But he does indeed record his protest and is no less impatient of Humean, associationist attempts to treat the self as a bundle of self-adhesive perceptual atoms. Transcendentalism, he says next, has the merit of recognizing the problem but serves only to pose it. What, then, is the 'basic principle of personal unity'? James concludes that the self, the I, is a present Thought which remembers and so appropriates past members of the stream of consciousness of which it is the present unit. This, he hopes, will account for the unity of the self and the difference between one self and another, without entering the realm of baseless speculation. The Me is the empirical person and the I the judging Thought.

Dewey admired and adopted the general approach but changed the emphasis. James's view could be deemed intellectualist, a case of *cogitat ergo sum*, so to speak. For Dewey there is no such thing as pure thought or Thought. Thought presupposes habit and involves action. Thinking, like all other intelligent activity, requires having already acquired an ability. An ability is a habit and its exercise depends on social relations. 'All life operates through a mechanism and the higher the form of life the more flexible the mechanism' (*HNC*, p. 70). 'Possession shapes and consolidates the "I" of philosophers. "I own therefore I am" expresses a truer psychology than the Cartesian "I think therefore I am" ' (*HNC*, p. 116). Dewey links James to Mead, by taking the I as the Thought in social action, imposing order on the experience of social life and at the same time adapting to it. As promised, the linking concept is that of habit.

For Dewey, man is a creature of habit. This sounds like the kernel of a stimulus-response theory, with Skinner-like implications for science, ethics and education. But Dewey has no such thing in mind. Habit is not just conditioned response but 'energy organised in certain channels' (*HNC*, p. 76). Nor is he writing a bore's charter, even though 'the nature of habit is to be assertive, insistent; self-perpetuating' (*HNC*, p. 58). In place of habit as passive routine, he offers us habits as ways of translating desire into intelligent action. 'All habits are demands for a certain kind of activity; they constitute the self' (*HNC*, p. 25). There is, in short, something inside the black box with energy and power to organize experience. The free man is the man who uses the power aright. The key to freedom is a simple but striking idea. The free man is the man of rational habits.

The phrase 'rational habits' wears an air of paradox. It is easy to think of rational action as action which is deliberately chosen under the conscious influence of good reasons. Equally, habitual actions are easily thought of as those done from mindless routine. So it is easy to oppose the rational and the habitual, with the result that large areas of life are transferred to the realm of the non-rational. I do not, for instance, drive my car rationally, if the test is that I must choose each and every action by reflecting consciously on what I should do next. This line of thought has its temptations. It has tempted the sociologist to argue that, since so little of life is rational,

61

he can ignore the notion of rationality in studying social action. It has tempted the moralist to urge us that we can be rational and free only if we become always critically self-aware. The common theme is that creatures of habit cannot be creatures of reason.

The snag is that a fully rational man, as just defined, would never get as far as his own front door. Each morning would find him barefoot in his bedroom, trying to decide which sock to put on first. Were others equally rational, civilization would collapse into paralysis, like some giant centipede told to put its best foot forward first. The error is to forget that freedom depends on skill and skill on habit. Motorist and mountaineer, call-girl and diplomat, yogi and commissar, juggler and philosopher can pursue their own good in their own way only if they are creatures of habit. The motorist literally and the others metaphorically need an unthinking control of their vehicles.

Such skills become, in the eyes of James or Dewey, parts of the self. But they do not make the self passive. They extend its activity and so extend the self. Yet this is not flatly true, since there are also deadening routines which stunt the self. 'What is necessary is that habits be formed which are more intelligent, more sensitively percipient, more informed with foresight, more aware of what they are about, more direct and sincere, more flexibly responsive than those now current' (*HNC*, p. 128). Man is a creature of habit but there are two kinds, not of habit, but of men. In some of us habits are divided against one another, personality is disrupted, the scheme of conduct is confused and disintegrated. In others released impulses are intelligently employed to form harmonious habits adapted to one another in a new situation. There is a nasty question here about the criteria for deciding when a habit is disruptive and to be overcome or when it is alerting and to be welcomed. Dewey is teasingly vague, as we shall complain later. Nevertheless, in so far as he can characterize good habits, the moral for education and for freedom stares us in the face.

Dewey takes the theoretical question about freedom a step further in a splendid essay entitled 'Philosophies of freedom'.[5] The essential problem of freedom, he says, is that of the relation of choice to unimpeded effective action. The key is that choice is not mere impulse, whim or will; nor is effective action mere power to do, as it is for an avalanche or earthquake. Choice 'signifies a capacity for deliberately changing preferences' (p. 276). It 'presents itself as one preference among and out of preferences; not in the sense of one preference already made and stronger than others but the formation of a new preference out of a conflict of preferences' (p. 276). Effective action is the enacting of rational preferences and 'freedom lies in the development of preferences into intelligent choices' (p. 296). Freedom is thus not the impulsive movement of an abstract, pre-social individual towards a given goal. It is the intelligent harmonizing of habits for the open-ended purpose of becoming an intelligent human being.

Why is this approach of living interest? The reason is epitomized by the strong actionist trends in social theory, bearing labels like phenomenology or ethnomethodology. Their root idea is that men do, or at least can, create their own social reality out of shared experience by acts of self-definition. It is not wholly a novel thought. Theories of the social contract made society the work of individuals. Notions of subjective and intersubjective meaning have long been the stock in trade of symbolic interactionism. Weber's use of meaning and action to explain social forms is as central to one grand line in sociology as Durkheim's emphasis on structures is to another. Recently, however, the idea of reality as a construct has become the rallying cry for a radical or humane approach to the social sciences, which rejects all these forms of 'positivism' in fields as different as history, physics, criminology or education. Although 'positivism' is a murky term in this context, I suppose it is meant to embrace all attempts to find law-like determinants of action external to human agents-*an-sich*. The villains are not only those, like Durkheim, who look directly to external and constraining social facts. They are also those who start with inner meanings but either take them as given and their construction as unproblematic or go on to explain them by appeal to social structures, thus merely lengthening the causal chain between structure and action. Weber is deemed finally as misguided as Durkheim. *Homo sociologicus* falls but the crown does not go to *homo psychologicus*, for psychology, too, has been a generalizing subject in search of law-like determinants of action, whereas strong actionism demands a theory to make human actors individual and autonomous.

Men are to be brought back in to explain the construction of reality. But what sort of men and how does their existence explain? By rejecting law-like determinants, strong actionism seems to abandon hope of ever explaining anything; and, by pouring scorn on the atoms of old liberalism and methodological individualism, seems to forfeit all chance of a self to sustain the construction of reality. Strong actionism, in short, threatens to be so radical that it dashes all hopes and has to end by borrowing eclectically from its opponents and hiding its debts in bombast. To escape this by now usual fate, it must take the I of the I-and-the-Me seriously, must produce an I discernibly sociological and must find a mode of explanation not law-like but still explanatory. Not even the kindest critic could suppose that it has yet succeeded.

Dewey's writings are therefore topical. He does indeed promise a coherent theory of the self in social action which is genuinely explanatory. But we should treat him gingerly. His mind runs on an intoxicating fluid which, as a recent advertisement for lager puts it, 'refreshes the parts which ordinary beers cannot reach'. This gives it high performance and huge output but makes for a certain casualness. For instance, we are told on page 42 of *Human Nature and Conduct* that habit means will, and on page 52 that will means habit. Such circularities are common and precision in one place is all too often cancelled by an embracing vagueness elsewhere. None the less the promise of a grand theory is there and I shall try to extract it by seeing what Dewey has to say about motive.

The ingredients of action, let us assume, are an environment, an occasion, an agent and an outcome. For instance, during a battle the arrival of enemy tanks sets the general a problem, which he solves by ordering his men back to the hills. What explains the general's action? That, no doubt, is an empirical question. But it is one only in so far as we already have a theory of action and motive which makes it one. Theories which perform this service can be grouped typically into the adaptive and the constructive. By an adaptive theory I mean one which treats the action as a conditioned response to the occasion; by a constructive theory one which takes the action as a step in the execution of a policy. Stimulus-response models are clear examples of the adaptive but they are not the only ones, nor are all adaptive theories behaviourist. Room can certainly be made for subjective and shared meanings. Allowance can be made for how the agent perceives his situation. Indeed, there is a place for the strong thesis that the very identities of the occasion and outcome depend on the description which the agent would give of them. The softer brands of actionism differ greatly from mechanical models. But, in echo of the radical critique of Weber, they, too, rely finally on causal determinants of action, usually beyond the realm of meanings and certainly beyond the actor-*an-sich*. This is, indeed, the litmus test for dividing actionisms into strong and weak and it places softer brands, like Weber's, in the adaptive category, for adaptive theories are those which try to explain *a tergo* with the aid of general laws. They are in one endlessly disputable word, determinist.

Dewey firmly denies that motives are causes working *a tergo* (*HNC*, p. 120):

> A motive does not exist prior to an act and produce it. It is an act *plus* a judgement on some element of it, the judgement being made in the light of the consequences of the act. . . . Instead then of saying that a man requires a motive in order to induce him to act, we should say that when a man is going to act he needs to know what he is going to do — what the quality of the act is in terms of consequences to follow. . . . A motive in short is simply an impulse viewed as a constituent in a habit, a factor in a disposition.

As so often, he gives us a broad idea of what he has in mind, while making it hard for us to pin him down. Broadly, questions of motive are to be addressed to acts as a whole, in order to elicit the actor's habits and judgment of consequences. But what precisely might this come to for the general and the enemy tanks? The general is no doubt recording his bold judgment of tactics for the sake of his memoirs. His batman is perhaps noting an impulse of fear as a constituent in the general's habit of cowardice. Both are following Dewey's instructions but they disagree not only about the actual motive but also about the sort of motive. What is Dewey to say?

The master's reply cannot be wholly satisfactory, given the casual way in which he makes disparate ideas share the same umbrella, but he is not left speechless. As in his account of freedom, he leaves the truth to turn on the degree to which the general's habits are intelligent. Impulse is an intermediary. It offers imagination and invention a chance, which they may or may not take. Impulse is needed to provoke thought but thought, 'born as the twin of impulse in every moment of impeded habit' (*HNC*, p. 171), can master impulse. If the general is a thoughtful man, he takes his chance and chooses freely by forming a new preference out of a conflict of preferences. If not, then the batman's explanation is the true one. In effect, therefore, Dewey has two incompatible theories of motive and resolves the conflict by giving each a different range of application. A motive is sometimes an impulse viewed as a constituent in a habit, sometimes an act plus a judgment on an element of the act. The former is the motive of an unenlightened man, the latter of a free man, and the implications Dewey draws for ethics, politics, education and democracy will be known to all his readers.

If Dewey rejects adaptive theories of motive for free action, does he then accept constructive ones? That depends on the further question of how far the explanation of action as a step in the execution of a policy involves postulating a self. In saying that the general pulled his troops back as a tactical means to a strategic end, what is assumed about the general? Hobbes defines freedom as 'the absence of all impediments to action which are not contained in the nature and intrinsical quality of the agent' and this is a question about the nature and intrinsical quality of the general. Dewey scorns a substantive self for William James's reasons and does not believe that human conduct displays the rational unity which is sometimes made the sign of a self. The truth is that 'there is no one ready-made self behind activities'. But there is still a self, the point being only that it is neither one nor ready-made. 'We arrive at the conceptions of motivation and interest only by the recognition that self-hood (except as it has encased itself in a shell of routine) is in process of making, and that any self is capable of including within itself a number of inconsistent selves, of unharmonised dispositions' (*HNC*, p. 137). Once again the key lies in habits and in the relation of habits to impulses (*HNC*, pp. 177ff.):

> Concrete habits do all the perceiving, imagining, recalling, judging, conceiving and reasoning. . . . Yet habit does not, of itself, know, for it does not of itself stop to think, observe or remember. Neither does impulse of itself engage in reflection or contemplation. It just lets go. . . . Without habit there is only irritation and confused hesitation. With habit alone there is a machine-like repetition, a duplicating recurrence of old acts. With conflict of habits and release of impulse there is conscious search.

The crucial phrase here is 'conscious search'. Those who reject an adaptive theory of action with its attempt to find determinants *a tergo* often propose a 'rational man' model instead. This rational man has clear goals and his actions are explained as rationally calculated means to his goals. If that is what constructive theories of action are about and if that is what explaining action as a step in the execution of a policy comes to, then Dewey rejects them too. An intelligent human being is consciously searching not only for means but also for goals. He is always in a state of becoming and the conscious search is a search for himself. The search is not a treasure hunt, however, since there is no pre-existent self to find. The search creates the self by bringing habits into harmony, thus translating the Thought into social action and constructing a man who is free and human.

The view is attractive but teasing and, having only a short time, I shall focus on the feature which most attracts and teases me. It is its notion of personal identity, designed to tempt philosophers and sociologists together. Such a virtue is rare, if not impossible. For philosophers discussing personal identity are far removed from sociologists discussing social identity and it is easy to suppose that wholly different concepts of identity are involved. Dewey would maintain, I fancy, that there is none the less a unitary concept to be had and would invite us to discern it in his translation of James's Thought into social action. Both parties are likely to object. Sociologists will complain that Dewey's free man, constantly seeking a harmonious self with no fixed goals or criteria of harmony, is chronically prone to anomie; that, where there is chronic anomie, there can be neither identity nor explanation. Philosophers will complain that Dewey has no notion of strict, numerical identity, without which any theory of personal identity falls. These are dissimilar complaints yet they share a demand for a fixed point in a qualitative world. If Dewey can meet the demand or show it importantly misguided, both parties will learn something to their advantage. My own view is that there ought to be a unitary concept, which would harness the two disciplines. Without going so far as to say what it is, I shall praise Dewey's attempt to find a harness and suggest what it lacks. To do more would only reveal my own ignorance and I offer criticism in no spirit of lordly scorn.

Philosophers and sociologists certainly seem to use different senses of 'identity'. The former typically seek logical and epistemological criteria by which persons can be identified and re-identified. The latter typically look for a theory of personality which will fuse psychology with role theory. It would be only a poor pun to say that both were interested in relations of identity, since logical relations like transitivity belong in a different universe from social relations like role partnership. There appears, in short, to be nothing of a philosophical interest which a crisis of identity is a crisis of. At the same time, however, neither discipline can be said to have emerged triumphant from its peculiar inquiries and there is at least this excuse for suggesting an alliance.

Of the philosophers' stock questions, I pick two: 'What is a person?' and 'What unites different stages of the same person?' As they are old questions, possible answers must pass old, severe tests. Essential attributes of a person and logical guarantees of continuing identity are demanded. For instance, if disembodied existence is possible, I cannot *be* my body, however sure we are that all persons are in fact embodied.

Memory is not a criterion, if two different people could possibly have the same memories, however well we know that it does not happen. Theories of identity are tested to destruction by *Gedankenexperimenten* and there are at present no undisputed survivors. What is a person? The concept of a person may be a primitive in relation to those of body and experience but we can hardly leave it at that and there is no easy riposte to James's attack on substantive, associationist or transcendental theories. Those who think persons essentially physical cannot yet specify the predicates which distinguish persons from other bodies. Those who think them essentially non-physical, cannot yet find a way to individuate consciousnesses. Similar (and, you may protest, equally tendentious) strictures apply to attempts at the other question. What unites different stages of the same person? Bodily continuity, however necessary, does not seem sufficient; non-physical criteria, however subtly they take account of mental life, do not seem to secure uniqueness. The hardy perennials can be posed in a minute and explored in an hour without making much advance on centuries of bafflement.

How tempting it is, then, to invoke some idea of social relations. Consciousness does not operate in a vacuum and bodies are just bodies unless the relations between them are endowed with shared meanings. James remarks: '*Properly speaking, a man has as many social selves as there are individuals who recognise him*' and adds that, more loosely, 'he has as many social selves as there are distinct *groups* about whose opinion he cares' (*Principles of Psychology*, p. 294, his italics). If we take the hint and look to sociology, we shall find at least two interesting lines of thought. One lies in structural role theory, where the self is externalized as the significant social behaviour of the individual and then absorbed into the roles attached to his social positions. The other follows the subjective path from symbolic interactionism until the self becomes images seen in the eyes of others, reflected to infinity. The snag from the philosophers' point of view, however, is that these lines do not yield notions of strict identity. A social position can by definition have more than one incumbent, so that each of us, even if in fact uniquely placed in some social system, is not guaranteed

Martin Hollis

uniqueness by citing the sum of his roles. Equally a person (or sort of social Leibnizian monad) defined by means of reflections in the eyes of others is logically unique, only if (*pace* Leibniz) some person not so defined is used as a fixed point of reference. Most philosophers will deem it neither essential to my being a person that I have social positions nor logically necessary to my being the person I am that my social relations are in sum unique to myself. The sociologist can elaborate until he is blue in the face, by adding to my role set the role sets of my role partners and of my role partners' role partners, throwing in the historical order in which I played my roles, listing my most significant experiences and even sneaking in mention of genotypes and phenotypes. These are all factors in my conduct and an intimate part of being me. But the philosopher is implacable. He demands strict identity, while the sociologist supplies something too lax to be identity at all.

Yet perhaps the philosopher is asking too much or the sociologist trying too little. In support of the latter alternative, there is a classic lacuna in role theory just where we might expect to learn who or what plays the roles. Readers of Erving Goffman, for instance, relish his nuanced accounts of how actors play their roles with varying styles and skill, at varying distance and for varying ends. But, noting that the social world is thus made to depend largely on the man in the masks, they look in vain for a theory of the self. To say, as Goffman does in *The Presentation of Self in Everyday Life*, that 'a self is a repertoire of behaviour appropriate to a given set of contingencies' is, however prettily epigrammatic, to speak in circles: for what makes the behaviour appropriate (or even a repertoire at all) is the ultimate character of the self and other selves, which the behaviour is being used to define. The same odd lacuna occurs among phenomenologists and others who would construct the social world from acts of self-definition expressed in shared meanings. Here an epistemological theory of the self is surely crucial, if individual men are to be justifiably presented as the creative *point d'appui* for the analysis of an intersubjective reality. But, apart from some hard sayings by Husserl, which his Anglo-Saxon descendants usually reject, none springs to mind.

70

Perhaps the gap could be filled, if the philosopher's demand for a notion of strict personal identity were taken seriously.

James and Dewey would take the other option, that, since reality is process, the philosopher is asking too much. There cannot be strict identity between distinct members of a series, and pragmatists, like Humeans, can relax. The Buddhist image of the self as a series of candles lit from the stub of the one before appealed to James. He analyses a person as a 'remembering Thought' and sets about the problem of personal identity by combining philosophy with psychology. Dewey, as we have seen, works in the same spirit but offers his idea of self-monitoring habits as the key to a door into sociology unlocked by Mead. James's I and Me, allied with Dewey's instrumentalism, tempt the stern philosopher to rethink his strict criteria of personal identity. Perhaps there is virtue in yielding. Indeed there certainly is, if A. J. Ayer is right in remarking:[6]

> If one speaks of the construction of objects out of the flux of experience, it is indeed natural to ask who does the constructing; and then it would appear that whatever self is chosen for this role must stand outside the construction; it would be contradictory to suppose that it constructed itself. But the metaphor of construction is here misleading. What is in question is the derivation of concepts, not the fabrication of the things to which the concepts apply. To 'construct' either the material or the spiritual self is to do no more than pick out the relations within experiences which make it possible for the concept of a self of this kind to be satisfied, and these relations exist whether or not we direct our attention to them.

The issue is too hard to settle at a stroke but I can at least open a line of thought. It is prompted by the reflection that a theory of human identity determines what should count as good reasons for action. I am not speaking of means-ends rationality with given ends and calculable means; nor of good reasons for pursuing ends which are in turn means to further ends. My question concerns good reasons for ultimate ends. The traditional answer is that we have ultimate interests deriving from our essential human nature. Hobbes and

Rousseau, for instance, were not simply issuing prescriptions off the tops of their heads with wild leaps from 'is' to 'ought'. They hold that whatever constitutes us as human beings is *eodem ipso* what we should preserve and develop. Their analysis of what is, no less than of what ought to be, rests on essential attributes of mankind. Such a strategy is out of fashion and is one reason often given for holding that traditional political theory is dead and buried. But, although buried, it is far from dead; for, even if human nature is specific to economic formations, modes of operant conditioning or given forms of life, these are still universal judgments about mankind. Even if a person is a body or a process with only qualitative identity, this is still a metaphysical thesis, to be judged, I would argue, by its claims to truth. Dewey, at any rate, holds both that his analysis of human nature is true and that it requires a democratic form of society, for democracy alone lets us cultivate rational habits and only by living a life of rational habits can we be truly human. Problems of personal identity are, for him, questions in what we might call the political philosophy of mind. *Human Nature and Conduct* is no careless title.

But his strength is also his downfall. The strength is that he works without given goals and refuses to talk the language of means and ends. The self is constituted by its habits, habits are malleable, means and ends are not distinguishable, criteria for guiding action are fluid and the self is, in short, always in a state of becoming. This has interesting implications both for the philosophy of mind and for the utilitarian social sciences, like neo-Classical economics. But there is a crucial snag. Rational habits are those 'more intelligent, more sensitively percipient . . . more flexibly responsive than those now current' (*HNC*, p. 128). If this is, in upshot, all Dewey can say, he faces an evident circularity. Rational habits are those which spread harmony among a man's discrepant selves; selves are discrepant when preferences are not turned into intelligent choices and so into effective action; choices are intelligent and action effective, when they let the self develop; the self develops when habits become more rational. There can be no exit and the charge of chronic anomie is justified. But although it is true that, where there is chronic anomie, there can be neither identity nor explanation, this is less a sociological fact than a philosophical consequence of having no independent criterion of harmony.

If Dewey's embarrassment is not total, it is because he is less noncommittal about ends than he makes out. On close inspection, he is seen to advance only the stock Enlightenment view that men have no goals *outside themselves*. He still assigns them the goal of being human.[7] It is a moving target, a more genial version of Hobbes's connection between Felicity and our perpetual and restless desire of power after power, that ceaseth only in death. But it is still a goal, translated by Dewey's theory of freedom into reasons for action under the spur of conflicting impulses. To this extent he is inconsistent. Nor will so vague an idea of what it is to be an intelligent human being stave off the critic who asks why we should pursue this ill-defined course. A fool satisfied is still a man and a satisfied man at that.

Turning a concept of a person into reasons for action is a hard alchemy and I do not pretend to have the philosophers' stone. But we can see what is needed, if we recall the old notion of *conatus*, signifying the endeavour of each thing to persist in its own being. According to Spinoza it is nothing else but the actual essence of the thing in question (*Ethics*, III, props VI, VII) and can be used to analyse resistance in passive things, freedom in active ones. Action which impedes *conatus* has its causes outside the agent, whereas rational action can be explained by the necessities of the agent's own nature. A true theory of essential human interests would apply descriptively to the conduct of free men and prescriptively to all. It would solve the old problem of identity by showing what was essential for each thing's being this particular individual member of its species. Then perhaps we would know which habits to cultivate, why only a fool is content to be satisfied and even which theory of education to apply.

While waiting for the philosophers' stone, we could do worse than read Spinoza. But that is not why I mention him. He appears here only to score a point about the rationality of ends. A system as elastic as Dewey's leaves no possible test for intelligent and harmonious habits. The trouble stems from an elastic criterion of personal identity. That is, I

73

submit, one reason why the self must stand outside the construction and why James was right to accept the need for a 'basic principle of personal unity', while rejecting Kant's claims to have found one. In final comment on Dewey's *Encyclopedia* article, with which we began, there have to be some limits to the modifiability of human nature, since we could otherwise have no reasons for action, and some limits to possible institutional change, since a change which destroys the identity of men in society also destroys all institutions. From these limits we can hope to derive the outline of a rational social policy. Experimental observation continues to have its vital place but only within an *a priori* theory which sets its scope, with due respect for uncertainty, given our theoretical ignorance.

Yet nothing in this conclusion favours the shopping centre against the general store. Sociologists who repair to Dewey will find a bargain analysis of rationality and its use in explaining the self in social action; philosophers will be tempted by theories of motive and human identity which make social relations relevant to an old enigma. These goods may not work perfectly but there are few and shoddier rivals on sale in the specialist shops up the road.

Notes

1 I am grateful to the John Dewey Foundation for instigating what has proved an absorbing task and to Bryan Heading and Quentin Skinner for their kind help and criticism.
2 Gordon W. Allport, 'Dewey's individual and social psychology', in P. A. Schlipp (ed.), *The Philosophy of John Dewey*, Tudor, New York, 1939. For Dewey's comments see esp. pp. 555f.
3 *Human Nature and Conduct*, part II, section IV, p. 125. This being the central text I am relying on, I shall refer to it as *HNC*. Page references are to the Modern Library edition, Henry Holt, New York, 1930.
4 These names for the divisions are the ones used in *Psychology: Briefer Course*, the shorter version of the theory first put forward in *The Principles of Psychology*, Henry Holt, 1890, ch. 10. My next page reference is to this chapter of *The Principles of Psychology*, Dover edn, 1950.
5 Originally in H.M. Kallen (ed.), *Freedom in the Modern World*, Coward McCann, NewYork, 1928, pp. 236–71; reprinted in John

Dewey, *Philosophy and Civilisation*, Minton Balch, New York, 1931, to which my page numbers refer.
6 *The Origins of Pragmatism*, Macmillan, 1968, part II, ch. 3, p. 261. Ayer lends distinguished support to James by working out an elegant qualitative theory of personal identity. There is also the interesting case put by Derek Parfit in 'Personal identity', *Philosophical Review*, vol. LXXX, no. 1, 1971.
7 See, for instance, 'Philosophies of freedom', reprinted in *Philosophy and Civilisation*, Minton Balch, New York, 1931, pp. 286ff. especially p. 287.

5   Democracy and education
Antony Flew

Perhaps my title ought to have been given in italics, for I shall
in the event be concerned mainly with the subject of democracy and education as, and in so far as, this is treated in one
particular Dewey book.[1] But he himself, in an autobiographi-
cal fragment, described that book as having been for many
years the source in which, not merely his ideal of education
for democracy, but his entire philosophy, 'was most fully
expounded'.[2] My treatment — like Caesar's Gaul — falls into
three parts. The first distinguishes at some length, and without direct reference to Dewey, three established areas of
meaning for the word 'democracy'. The second, and by far
the most substantial, examines Dewey's two proposed criteria
for an ideal society; which would, he affirms, be democratic.
The third and shortest notices one or two educational recommendations not very closely tied to the central theme of this
particular book. All three parts, and the notes thereto, make
various more or less unfriendly references to *Education for
Democracy*,[3] a widely circulated and, presumably, influential work by a group of Penguin Educationalists. The relevance
of these references is as links between Dewey and current
debate.

1   Preliminary inquiries about democracy

Anyone who once long ago sat at the feet of 'the implacable
professor', and who nevertheless undertakes now to read a
lecture entitled 'Democracy and Education', must begin with
some apology; for did not John Austin give 'democracy' as
his paradigm case of a 'notoriously useless word'?[4] Certainly
it is both ambiguous and vague. Yet on neither of these two
different counts can it be abandoned as futile. I shall in a
moment myself be urging that we have to distinguish at least
three main areas of meaning. But that a word has two senses,

76

or more, is never by itself sufficient reason to conclude that it is even desirable, much less practical, in one or more of these present senses to replace it by another. Nor would it be sensible to propose that we should, especially in our talk about matters of the highest importance, dispense with all words which are in any direction vague.

At first hearing that last suggestion may indeed appear obviously sensible. Yet a short pause for thought will reveal that it must be utterly impossible to do without either precise expressions or vague expressions. We have to have ways of saying, for instance, both 'four o'clock on the dot' and 'some time in the middle of the afternoon'. More immediately to the present point, many of the most important of all differences happen to be differences of degree. They are, that is to say, differences in which the clear-cut paradigm cases at one extreme are linked to the clear-cut paradigm cases at the opposite extreme by a spectrum of actual or possible, more or less marginal, cases in the middle. Until and unless we choose to draw some arbitrary line, therefore, the terms employed to characterize such opposites cannot but be vague: 'To remove vagueness is to outline the penumbra of a shadow: the line is there after we have drawn it; but not before.'[5]

Yet nothing could be more wrong, nor more common, than to assume, or even to say, that all differences of degree are *mere* differences of degree, for, defined as we have just defined them, these supposed 'mere differences of degree' include many if not most humanly vital differences: the differences, for example, between youth and age; between riches and poverty; between sanity and insanity; and between a free society and one in which — as used to be said of Imperial Germany — everything which is not forbidden is compulsory.

(a) By the people

In the first of the three areas of meaning to be distinguished the word 'democratic' is applied to methods of making state or, more generally, group decisions. If some group as a whole takes decisions by majority vote, then that is democratic. So, too, are institutions under which decisions are made by delegates, representatives, or other officers who can in due course be voted out.

Two things in this indication of the first area of meaning require further explanation in the present context. The first is my emphasis on voting out, not voting in. For today's world this is of great topical importance. In the newly created states of formerly British Africa, for instance, most of the original regimes were established as the result of tolerably presentable elections. But nearly all of these regimes then jettisoned their claims to democratic legitimacy by proceeding in fairly short order to take steps to ensure that it should be impossible — in that good old phrase — 'to vote the scoundrels out'. The second thing to notice is my studiously non-paternalist emphasis upon what voters do actually want; as against what they may be supposed to need, or what it may or may not be in their interests to have.

(b) For the people

The importance of that second emphasis emerges more fully as we move to the second area of meaning. Consider such increasingly common political labels as 'People's Democratic Republic of the Yemen', 'Democratic Republic of North Vietnam', or 'Somali Democratic Republic'. Those of us who still remain devoted to democracy as first conceived may too quickly put down such employments of the hooray word 'democratic' as just so many more specimens of sickeningly mendacious propaganda. But that is not the whole story, and the other part is for us the more important.

Two authoritative statements will bring out what that other part is. My first witness is Janos Kadar, addressing the Hungarian National Assembly on 11 May 1957, one year after the friendly neighbourhood Soviet tanks installed him in office:[6]

> The task of the leaders is not to put into effect the wishes and will of the masses. . . . The task of the leaders is to accomplish the interests of the masses. Why do I differentiate between the will and the interests of the masses? In the recent past we have encountered the phenomenon

of certain categories of workers acting against their interests.

As my second witness I call the late Abdul Kharume, First Vice-President of Tanzania. Mr Kharume, who has since been assassinated, was, as his Afro-Shirazi Party in Zanzibar still is, strongly influenced by advisers from the German Democratic Republic. Referring to a recent round-up of the unemployed in Dar-es-Salaam, he said:[7]

Our government is democratic because it makes its decisions in the interests of, and for the benefit of, the people. I wonder why men who are unemployed are surprised and resentful at the Government . . . sending them back to the land for their own advantage.

We can, therefore, distinguish a second political sense of the word 'democratic'. It is, presumably, derivative from the first. The crux is suggested by Janos Kadar, and spelt out by Abdul Kharume.

(Parenthetically: those interested in the history of ideas will see Rousseau as, whether willy or nilly, one of the main intellectual forebears of this second concept of democracy; for Rousseau's often deceived but never corrupted General Will is always upright, and necessarily directed to the collective good, while the notorious fact that it is not to be reliably discovered, either in the hurly-burly of contested elections, or through the deliberations of representative assemblies, gives such a doctrine strong appeal to all who think of themselves as belonging to a party of the vanguard.)[8]

(c) Of the people

The third area of meaning has, so far as I can see, no essential connection with the political. The big *Oxford English Dictionary* glosses, with little enthusiasm: 'In modern use often more vaguely, denoting a social state in which all have equal rights, without hereditary, or arbitrary, differences of rank or privilege.' Thus we may describe the social-life arrangements of some organization, which is perhaps in working hours hierarchical and authoritarian, as thoroughly democratic: the managing director plays football under the captaincy of an apprentice; and so on.

Using the word 'democratic' in this sort of sense, an institution which is in its recruitment highly selective, and itself perhaps in many ways privileged, may properly be described as democratic; providing only that recruitment to it is socially open, and not determined by 'hereditary, or arbitrary, differences of rank or privilege'. This granted it becomes urgently topical to press upon all those who employ that currently most fashionable term of abuse, 'elitist', the question: first, whether, for them, all selection and all segregation on the basis of any form of achievement or capacity is elitist, and therefore bad; or, second, whether, for them, the epithet 'elitist' is pretty well synonymous with the word 'undemocratic' employed in a sense of this third kind. About this I will now say in passing only that, if and in so far as someone is inclined to answer 'Yes' to the first of these questions, then that person — though 'in the darkness of these times', probably accepted as an educationalist — begins with that answer to take up arms against all education, all quality, all culture, and all civilization.

There seems, as I have already suggested, to be no logically necessary connection between the present third area of meaning for the word 'democratic' and either of the first two; although it is no doubt true that groups which are democratic in the first way, or even in the second, will in fact tend to be so also in the third. Thus Alexis de Tocqueville has a chapter with the prematurely Gaullist title: 'Democratic social conditions of the Anglo-Americans'.[9] Yet he does not suggest that these conditions are more than contingently connected with the possibility of upset elections — much less with the absolutism of a totalitarian socialist party of the vanguard.

The contributors to *Education for Democracy* are operating mainly in this third area; although several are obviously committed to the first, and some to the second, sort of political democracy.[10] For the thrust of the whole book is towards a universal, compulsory, comprehensive system; with the absolute minimum of either setting or streaming. Thus one of the two editors concludes his own contribution: 'Without absorbing the independent, and particularly the public schools, into the state system, any talk of education for democracy remains a mockery' (*ED*, p. 88).

2 Dewey's concept of the ideal society

Let us now, a little late in the day, open our Dewey. The first sentence of his Preface reads: 'The following pages embody an endeavour to detect and state the ideas implied in a democratic society and to apply these ideas to the problems of the enterprise of education' (*DE*, p. iii). We might, therefore, expect forthwith to proceed to some explanation of what Dewey proposes to mean by the word 'democracy'; to be followed perhaps by an account of the relations, or lack of relations, between this meaning and other established meanings. In fact we do not. The first reference to democracy occurs in chapter 7. Nowhere is there any treatment of other interpretations as such.

In chapter 7, under the title 'The democratic conception in education', Dewey seeks 'a measure for the worth of any given mode of social life. . . . The problem is to extract the desirable traits of forms of community life which actually exist, and employ them to criticize undesirable features and suggest improvement' (*DE*, p. 83). He picks out two such traits, happily discovering that these 'are precisely what characterize the democratically constituted society' (*DE*, p. 87). What they are is positive scores on the questions: 'How numerous and varied are the interests which are consciously shared? How full and free is the interplay with other forms of association?' (*DE*, p. 83).

(a) The status of Dewey's criteria

Sometimes the characteristics thus specified do seem to be being construed as if they were elements in a definition of 'democracy'. But these are occasions when Dewey is even further than usual from any consideration of possible principles and procedures of political decision-making. Indeed he scarcely could have thought, when he did thus happen to have our first area of meaning in mind, that there is any

81

logically necessary connection between that and these two most-favoured characteristics. The absolute maximum which could be said on these lines is that his two criteria provide useful contingent indications — as someone might suggest that we could arrange countries on a scale of the more or less easy for their own citizens to get out of and for others to get into. But while we could perhaps do something of this sort with Dewey's second criterion, there would seem to be no comparable mileage to be got out of the first.

So I take it that we ought to consider these criteria, neither as tests for the presence of democracy in any political sense, nor as contributions to the elucidation of such a sense, but rather — as after all, Dewey himself suggested earlier on the same page — as offering a comprehensive index of all the excellences of 'an ideal society' (*DE*, p. 83). If there is any necessary connection between Dewey's ideal and democracy, then it will be not with the first or second but the third area of meaning.

Two of the first things to remark about Dewey's treatment, both in *Democracy and Education* and elsewhere, are, therefore: first, how little he has to say about electoral politics; and, second, how, even when he does say that little, he never seems to notice that his own usual understanding of the word 'democratic' runs somewhere far from its primary employment. The most striking but still partial exception which I have found to this general rule is in the final chapter, 'Democracy and education' in *Schools of Tomorrow*. The passage begins: 'Our famous brief definition of democracy, as government of the people, by the people, for the people. . . .' It continues for many pages in that understanding.[11]

The same first two remarks apply with almost equal force to *Education for Democracy*. Several contributors do in one way or another reveal personal political commitments either to 'participatory democracy' or to 'democratic centralism'. But almost no attempt is made there to relate educational proposals to such political understandings of the word. Neither do the authors show much appreciation of any need to explain their own present preferred usage, nor to relate it to current alternatives. Nanette Whitebread, for instance, presses her boo and hooray stops with undiscerning and

uncritical abandon: 'Government vacillation . . . has reflected
the struggle between democracy and elitism, in which the
latter has been aided by pressure to restrict spending in a pre-
dominantly private, capitalist economy'; and, 'Successive
governments have been guilty of anti-democratic mismanage-
ment of teacher supply' (*ED*, p. 176).

Since she, like most of her fellow contributors, typically
contrasts democracy with elitism we can presume that she
shares their primary present concern with our third area of
meaning. But, as neither she nor any of the others ever distinguishes senses, we are disappointed of answers to our fundamental questions. For instance: what precisely is the objection
to independent schools? Is it really an objection not to independence but to non-academic selectivity; an objection which
could, therefore, be met by possible arrangements to ensure
that their admissions took no account of 'hereditary, or arbitrary, differences of rank or privilege'? Or is it an entirely
different objection, essentially socialist, to independence as
such? If we did get an answer it would be, I guess, that
Nanette Whitebread and most of her fellow Penguin Educationalists object on both grounds. They are, that is: both — as
socialists — against any independence from state or other collective public ownership and control; and also — as a kind of
educationalist, if not perhaps of educator — against selection
even on the most purely academic criteria. But these two
objections are quite different. They need to be separately
stated, and distinguished.

(b) Formal rather than material criteria

Returning to Dewey's two measures 'for the worth of any
given mode of social life', the next thing to notice is that
they are both, in a sense to be explained, purely formal.
Both, Dewey says (*DE*, pp. 86–7),

> point to democracy. The first signifies not only more
> numerous and more varied points of shared common in-
> terest, but greater reliance upon the recognition of mutual
> interests as a factor of social control. The second means
> not only freer interaction between social groups (once

isolated so far as intention could keep up separation) but change in social habit — its continuous readjustment through meeting the new situations produced by varied intercourse.

The key expressions here are 'more varied . . . shared common interest', 'freer interaction', and 'change . . . continuous readjustment'. They all refer to formal characteristics. Nothing is said about the substantial questions: the quality of the shared interests, the nature of the results of the interaction, or the direction of the change. Pure formality is by no means always a fault. Thus it is not, though it has often been said to be, a fault in the conception of freedom, as freedom from, that it is negative; that it says nothing of what that freedom is to be used to do. Nor is it a fault in the primary conception of democracy that it refers only to procedures for taking or reversing decisions, not to the content or outcome of decisions taken. But it is at least odd, and to my mind also a fault, to offer such purely formal characteristics as comprehensive criteria of social desirability: 'The problem is to extract the desirable traits of forms of community life . . . and employ them to criticize undesirable features . . .'; and, 'From these two traits we derive our standard' (*DE*, p. 83).

The nature of this oddity will be better appreciated if we compare Dewey's position with that of those for whom equality, as opposed to any kind of quality, is an independent value — perhaps even the supreme value;[12] for equality is, in the present sense, a formal characteristic: it recruits a substantial associate only when we specify at what absolute level and in respect of what the equality does or should obtain. Furthermore: if, and in so far as, equality is accepted as an independent value, then, and to that extent, the way is open for the sacrifices to the pursuit of equality of other and more substantial goods. The size of the sacrifices actually required will, of course, depend: both on the weight given to equality relative to those other values; and on what goods might in the particular situation in fact be obtained. But suppose people are not willing to accept any sacrifices of other possible goods for the sake of more equality; then, it follows necessarily, equality is not for them an independent value.

Among the immediate consequences of the elementary analysis of the previous paragraph are that this commitment necessarily involves some degree of willingness: both to hold back, or even to depress, the better off with no compensating advantage to the worse off; and to hold back, or even to depress, everyone for the sake of more equality than might otherwise be achieved.

Having thus emphasized unlovely implications of the single-minded pursuit of distributional equality, both charity and justice require me to notice at once that for many of those who insist upon talking as if all inequality is self-evidently bad, such equality is nevertheless not really an independent value. Concern for it is instead derived from other value commitments which are for them more fundamental.[13] Nor indeed is Dewey in the end devoted to the mere numerousness and variety of interests as such. These indices serve and can serve as criteria for the general excellence of a society only because, he persuades himself, the more numerous and the more varied the interests, then, as a matter of fact, the better (by other but here unspecified standards). He writes (*DE*, p. 83):

> If we apply these considerations to, say, a criminal band, we find that the ties which hold its members together are few in number. . . . If we take, on the other hand, the kind of family life which illustrates the standard, we find that there are material, intellectual, aesthetic interests in which all participate.

Acceptance of the criteria proposed must also be facilitated by a certain carelessness as to what they are supposed to be. The first question as originally proposed read: 'How numerous and varied are the interests which are consciously shared?' (*DE*, p. 83). Yet in the 'Summary' at the end of that same chapter we are told that the first of 'The two points selected by which to measure the worth of a form of social life' was 'the extent in which the interests of a group are shared by all its members' (*DE*, p. 99).

(c) The implications of these criteria

In examining these measures 'for the worth of any given mode

85

of social life' I first noticed that, though Dewey is forever talking of his great society as democratic, this book contains almost no references to any kind of political democracy.[14] Nor does Dewey make much attempt either to relate his ideals to any such established notion or to differentiate them therefrom. Second, I pointed out that his indices are curiously formal. This formality would perhaps be no fault if Dewey were attempting some account of democracy in an existing sense. But it is very odd when what he is proposing is a comprehensive index of all the excellences of 'an ideal society'. My third concern is with the actual implications of the criteria recommended.

For Dewey, we recall, the key questions are: 'How numerous and varied are the interests which are consciously shared? How full and free is the interplay with other forms of association?' (*DE*, p. 83). Since these are supposed to be criteria of democracy (*DE*, p. 87),

> A democracy is more than a form of government, it is primarily a mode of associated living, of conjoint communicated experience. The extension in space of the number of individuals who participate is an interest so that each has to refer his own action to that of others, and to consider the action of others to give point and direction to his own, is equivalent to the breaking down of those barriers of class, race, and national territory which kept men from perceiving the full import of their activity.

The second of those two sentences contains a characteristic emphasis upon what we have to recognize as the third area of meaning. It also makes remarkable suggestions, that the ideal society has an inherent drive to become a world community, and maybe that the bigger and more populous the community the better, too. The first sentence spells out the first criterion. G. H. Bantock recently drew attention to the 'strong equalizing tendencies in the direction of sameness' in this 'asserted need for an increased community of experience open to all'.[15] But Bantock missed the opposite tendency, towards diversification, which Dewey discovers in his second criterion; for the passage just quoted — a passage cited by Bantock too — continues (*DE*, p. 87):

These more numerous and more varied points of contact denote a greater diversity of stimuli to which an individual has to respond; they consequently put a premium on variation in his action. They secure a liberation of powers which remain suppressed as long as the incitations to action are partial as they must be in a group which in its exclusiveness shuts out many interests.

But even if we do concede that this opposite tendency really is implicit in the original insistence upon maximum 'interplay with other forms of association', there is no getting away from the truth of Bantock's contention that 'there are strong pressures towards equality of *outcome* in the work of John Dewey';[16] for if associations are good and democratic in so far as their members share numerous and varied interests, and if education for democracy is to be a matter of concentrating on the development of various but always shared interests, then the variety of those shared interests, and the scope for independent individual development, necessarily must be limited correspondingly. It must, that is to say, be limited by and to whatever happens to be the maximum attainable either by the least richly talented or by the modal majority.

Maybe Dewey himself would have been unhappy about the full force of these implications. But he never comes to terms in this context with the truth that people vary enormously in all natural endowments. He is not so foolish as to deny the fact that we do. Yet he somehow contrives not to notice its relevance to his first criterion of social merit. He writes (*DE*, p. 90):

We cannot better Plato's conviction that an individual is happy and society well organized when each individual engages in those activities for which he has a natural equipment, nor his conviction that it is the primary office of education to discover this equipment to its possessor and train him for its effective use. But progress in knowledge has made us aware of the superficiality of Plato's lumping of individuals and their powers into a few sharply marked off classes; it has taught us that original capacities are indefinitely numerous and variable.

Fair enough. Our natural endowments vary in indefinitely many dimensions, and these variations are continuous rather than separated by gulfs between sharply different categories. But these are no reasons for denying: either that the distances between the actual extremes in any of these dimensions may be — as they in fact very often are — enormous; or that there cannot be — as again there in fact very often are — substantial average differences in respect of some particular natural endowment as between one group of people and another. Dewey does not draw either of these two negative conclusions, explicitly. They do not follow. What he does do is simply to proceed as if he had. He recognizes no tension between the tendency towards diversification, which he discovers in his second criterion, and the drive towards an equality of outcome, which is built into the first; and he takes it that the facts show that 'social organization means utilization of the specific and variable qualities of individuals, not stratification by classes' (*DE*, p. 91).

Allow — as Dewey would certainly wish, and as must be true — that any defection from ideal equality of opportunity wastes talent.[17] Still a form of social utilization which makes the fullest use 'of the specific and variable qualities of individuals' does not thereby preclude 'stratification by classes'; for even the sort of group which sociologists would be prepared to admit as a social class can in its recruitment be wide open to the rising talents. It can be open downwards too, to the lack of talents. To the extent that actual social classes are in fact thus open, both upwards and downwards, and to the extent that any relevant natural endowments are heritable, the children of these open social classes are bound to become as such members of a group of people distinguishable from other groups of people by an average difference in respect of those particular endowments.[18]

Two or three paragraphs back I suggested, with charitable intent, that Dewey might himself have been unhappy with the implications which Bantock and I both want to underline. No one, after all, should overlook the likelihood that he shared with us readers at least some difficulties in determining exactly, or even not very exactly, what it was that he did want to say. Yet he does himself later apply his criteria in ways that I do find disturbing. For instance (*DE*, p. 122):

> the idea of perfecting an 'inner' personality is a sure sign
> of social divisions. What is called inner is simply that which
> does not connect others, which is not capable of full and
> free communication. What is termed spiritual culture has
> usually been futile, with something rotten about it, just be-
> cause it has been conceived as a thing which a man might
> have internally — and therefore exclusively. What one is as
> a person is what one is as associated with others, in a free
> give and take of intercourse.

Without those carefully chosen and worked examples
which Dewey seems never to provide we are not, perhaps,
entitled to feel sure precisely what this polemic against the
private is intended to condemn. There could be little educational point or profit here in a Wittgensteinian onslaught
upon the (logically) private as such. It is, nevertheless, to
be noted that this interpretation could not be dismissed
out of hand as a total anachronism, for in discussing how
words get understood, Dewey wrote: 'they acquire the same
meaning with the child which they have with the adult
because they are used in a common experience of both' (*DE*,
p. 15).

The obvious alternative interpretation is to construe Dewey
as validly inferring from the two proposed criteria of social
excellence, and in particular from the first, the to my mind
appalling moral that everything (contingently) private is
divisive, rotten, and intolerable. Remembering those rudi-
mentary anticipations of the later Wittgenstein we might see
Dewey as reinforced in his determination to maintain this
embargo by a rather murky suspicion that what he deplores
must in any case be somehow even logically vicious.

Yet does he really want to ban all private or solitary activities, all going apart from or against the collective? I think
here among other things of recent remarks by one of Dewey's
own most distinguished pupils: 'Possessing moral courage
himself, Dewey took it for granted that others had it'; and
'The gabble in the academies about the vice of conformism
is empty and meaningless. . . . What we must cherish is not
agreement or disagreement but intellectual independence,

the courage to hold a position on the strength of the evidence
no matter what the baying of the crowds.'[19]

(d) What is the appeal of these criteria?

Having, in the previous section, looked at implications of
Dewey's proposed criteria of social excellence, it is now time
to ask, in the fourth, how these could have seemed to him so
obviously right. The clue lies in a sentence which connects
two passages already quoted much earlier (*DE*, p. 83):

> The problem is to extract the desirable traits of forms of
> community life which actually exist, and employ them to
> criticize undesirable features and suggest improvement.
> Now in every social group whatever, even in a gang of
> thieves, we find some interest held in common, and we
> find a certain amount of interaction and cooperative inter-
> course with other groups. From these two traits we derive
> our standard.

From this it is easy to pick out the nerve of the argument.
If and in as much as interests held in common, and a certain
amount of interaction and cooperative intercourse with other
groups, are defining characteristics of a society, then and for
that reason the greater the degree in which any society mani-
fests these characteristics the more of a society it is, and so
the better it is as a society. It is not a sound argument, not-
withstanding that arguments of this same form seem to have
persuaded many of the wise and good. Nor is it plausible to
suggest that the second of the two proposed characteristics
is defining. The argument is not sound, since you might as
well say that, because a smoked salmon is by definition
smoked, it must be a better smoked salmon the more smoked
it is. The suggestion is not plausible, since there is no contradiction in speaking of a completely closed and isolated
society, all of whose members believe — what by the hypothesis I hereby stipulate to be in fact the case — that it is the
sole society there is.

Although the argument would be no better, the suggestion
would be more plausible if 'interaction and cooperative intercourse within the group itself' were to be substituted for

'interaction and cooperative intercourse with other groups'. Indeed I cannot think of any reason, apart from a general North American prejudice in favour of extraversion, why Dewey should have introduced this reference to — as it were — foreign affairs. An introverted version of Dewey's second criterion might, however, be put forward as essential to the idea of social relationship.

Back in chapter 1 Dewey himself explained the logical liaisons between the notions of community, communication, and consensus (*DE*, pp. 4—5):

> Men live in a community in virtue of the things which they have in common; and communication is the way in which they come to possess things in common. . . . Individuals do not . . . compose a social group because they all work for a common end. The parts of a machine work . . . for a common result, but they do not form a community. If, however, they were all cognizant of the common end[,] and all interested in it[,] so that they regulated their specific activity in view of it, then they would form a community. But this would involve communication. . . . Consensus demands communication (commas supplied).

It is, I believe, both true and fundamental that both community and consensus presuppose communication — providing always that 'communication' is not construed as necessitating a developed language. This is no place for attempting a full analysis of such notions. It is sufficient and perhaps necessary simply to recall Hume's example of two people agreeing, without words and without contract, to row a boat together.[20] The minimum of communication required for such primal social acts is some mutual awareness, combined with some mutual recognition of the possibility of reaction one to the other: 'There is', as Dewey says, 'more than a verbal tie between the words common, community and communication' (*DE*, p. 4).

But it is quite another thing, and much more disputatious, to say that a group of people cannot constitute a community, and perhaps cannot even be in social relationships at all, unless they have and are cognizant of a common end, are all interested in it, and all consciously regulate their activities with this common end in mind. To insist on this would, surely, be an arbitrary exercise in high redefinition.[21] It would also be vastly to overestimate the actual role of such shared intentions in social living, for most people do not consciously decide whether to become or to remain members of a society, as opposed to living as hermits. Hence they have little occasion to ask themselves what are the common ends of their society, and how far they are themselves interested in these supposed collective purposes.

We cannot in such contexts too often remind ourselves of the importance of the unintended consequences of intended action. Dewey, I think, never went to school with Bernard de Mandeville or with the great men of the Scottish Enlightenment. So let us ponder again some famous words of Adam Smith — words so often drowned by the uncomprehending ridicule of those whose socialism blinds them to an essential of social science:

> As every individual . . . endeavours as much as he can . . .
> to employ his capital . . . that its produce may be of the
> greatest value; every individual necessarily labours to
> render the annual revenue of the society as great as he can.
> He generally, indeed, neither intends to promote the pub-
> lic interest, nor knows how he is promoting it . . . he
> intends only his own gain, and he is in this, as in many
> other cases, led by an invisible hand to promote an end
> which was no part of his intention.

Furthermore, Smith continues, it is not[22]

> always the worse for the society that it was no part of it.
> By pursuing his own interest he frequently promotes that
> of the society more effectually than when he really intends
> to promote it. I have never known much good done by
> those who affected to trade for the public good.

3 Universal theory and particular stances

I have devoted most of this paper to Dewey's notion of democracy, and its implications for education. Since I am dealing with the book *Democracy and Education*, and since these are the things which that book is supposed to be about, it would seem to be a natural and proper distribution. But the consequence of this concentration is that I have been operating mainly in what I cannot help but see as a disaster area. This raises for me a question which always comes to mind whenever I attend to any of Dewey's philosophical work. The question is, brutally, how someone who seems to have been such a poor philosopher, and a poor writer, can be so admired by former students of the quality of Ernest Nagel and Sidney Hook?

A similar question arises about the Australian philosopher, John Anderson — for those of us who can judge him only by his published work have to rate this as much inferior to that of such distinguished pupils as John Mackie, John Passmore, or David Armstrong. I suggest that in both cases the explanation lies in the face-to-face impact of a personality, and in a lifetime of commitments on innumerable public issues. Whether or not I am right in my two scandalous judgments of philosophical calibre, and in my suggested answers to the consequent questions, something does need to be said about some other recommendations which are, in *Democracy and Education*, presented, or misrepresented, as derivations from a general theory of education for democracy. Many of these must have had, and have, much wider appeal than that theory; although the appeal of some is not, of course, to the same people as the appeal of others.

(a) The unintended in education

It is, for instance, remarkable that someone so inclined when traversing the higher reaches of theory to exaggerate the importance of intention should, reverting to concrete educational situations, maintain a wholly salutary emphasis upon unintended learning and often unintended teaching: '. . . this "unconscious influence of the environment" is so subtle and pervasive that it affects every fibre of character and mind'; and 'Adults are naturally most conscious of directing the conduct of others when they are immediately aiming so to do. . . . But the more permanent and influential modes of control are those which operate from moment to moment continuously without such deliberate intention on our part' (*DE*, pp. 18, 26).[23]

(b) Confusion about the social

Notice next, and this has more connecting with his official theme, that Dewey rejects the suggestion 'that an individual's tendencies are naturally purely individualistic or egoistic, and thus anti-social'. He points out that we are all 'also interested . . . in entering into the activities of others and taking part in conjoint and cooperative doings' (*DE*, pp. 23, 26). Unfortunately he makes no distinction between: what is anti-social, in the sense of damaging to others; and what is anti-social, in the sense of opposed to all essentially social institutions. He is also inclined to mistake it that whatever is in that fundamental sense essentially social must be collectively directed and controlled. Dewey thus falls into two nowadays extremely popular misconceptions: that the private is necessarily anti-social, in the sense of damaging to others; and that the social, in either sense, is necessarily collectivist.

For instance, meditating applications of 'electrical science . . . to means of communication, transportation, lighting of cities and houses, and more economical production of goods', he comments (*DE*, p. 201; italics original):

> These are *social* ends . . . and if they are too closely associated with notions of private profit, it is because . . . they have been deflected to private uses: a fact which puts upon the school the responsibility of restoring their connection . . . with public scientific and social interests.

Wait a minute: the fact that certain essentially social arrangements make private profits possible has no tendency to show that these arrangements are in the ordinary and superficial sense anti-social, or that they do not at the same time fulfil all sorts of other worthy public and private purposes; and, furthermore, I want to say: not only are Dewey's implicit arguments for socializing conclusions unsound as arguments; but there is also in the public interest in fact a great deal to be said for private profit — especially perhaps when opposed to today's most favoured actual alternative, public loss.

(c) Collectivism and centralization

Dewey's collectivist inclinations were not at this time specifically statist.[24] Certainly he did always support the American public schools — 'this magnificent institution' — against all private alternatives: he speaks with enthusiasm of 'that growing and finally successful warfare against all the influences, social and sectarian, which would prevent or mitigate the sway of public influence over private ecclesiastical and class interests'.[25] Certainly he moves much too quickly from the need for 'the support of the state' to 'a movement for publicly conducted and administered schools'. The unreconstructed liberal will wish that Dewey had attended to the warnings of John Stuart Mill: 'One thing must be strenuously insisted upon; that the government must claim no monopoly for its education either in the lower or the higher branches. . . .'[26]

But we should also remember: that the system which Dewey favoured so strongly is in fact remarkably decentralized; that it appears to have room for a lot of selection on academic grounds; and that one of its units has recently become the first educational authority in the world to introduce vouchers as an instrument for extending effective family choice. All these things must give pause to anyone hoping to recruit Dewey as a posthumous patron of the enragés of *Education for Democracy*.

(d) Philosophical insights and the teaching situation

Much of Dewey's appeal to those who really care about teaching surely lies in such excellent down-to-earth recommendations as: 'There must be more actual material, more *stuff*, more appliances, and more opportunities for doing things. . . .' (*DE*, p. 156: italics original). This particular recommendation is presented as the outcome of philosophizing independent of the main official theme of the book. The cruces are the priority of knowing-how over knowing-that, and the wrongness of any receptive blank-paper account of the acquisition of knowledge: 'The knowledge which comes first to persons, and that remains most deeply ingrained, is knowledge of *how to do* . . .' (*DE*, p. 184: italics original); while

'It would seem as if five minutes' unprejudiced observation of the way an infant gains knowledge would have sufficed to overthrow the notion that he is engaged in receiving impressions . . .' (*DE*, p. 271).

(e) Dewey and Whitman's democracy

Another excellent recommendation is that it is easier to make economic than political history come alive for children. But here we return to the main theme: 'Economic history is more human, *more democratic*, and hence more liberalizing than political history' (*DE*, pp. 215—16: italics supplied). It is my cue for a final suggestion. The democracy of which Dewey talked, Walt Whitman sang:

Yet utter the word Democratic, the word En-Masse.[27]

I speak the password primeval, I give the sign of democracy,
By God! I will accept nothing which all cannot have their
    counterpart of on the same terms.[28]

It is in Democracy — (the purport and aim of all the past)
It is in the life of one man or one woman today — the
    average man of today.[29]

I heard that you asked for something to prove this puzzle
    to the new world,
And to define America, her athletic Democracy,
Therefore I send you my poems that you behold in them
    what you wanted.[30]

Notes

1 *Democracy and Education* by John Dewey, New York, Macmillan, 1916. All references to *DE* below will be to the 1964 third printing of the 1961 Macmillan Paperbacks edition.
2 Quoted, with no reference given, by John L. Childs, 'The educational philosophy of John Dewey', in P. A. Schiipp (ed.), *The Philosophy of John Dewey*, New York, Tudor, 2nd edn, 1951, p. 417. The phrase is not to be found in any contribution by Dewey to the Library of Living Philosophers, for in this case there is no Autobiography, but only a Biography compiled with his help by his daughters.
3 David Rubinstein and Colin Stoneman (eds), *Education for Demo-*

cracy, Harmondsworth and Baltimore, Penguin Education, 2nd edn, 1972. All references to *ED*, below, will be to this edition.

4 See his *Sense and Sensibilia*, Oxford, Clarendon, 1962, p. 127. The whole sentence reads: 'There are, however, a few notoriously useless words — "democracy", for instance — uses of which are always liable to leave us in real doubt what is meant; and here it seems reasonable enough to say that the *word* is vague' (italics original).

5 Who first said this, and where?

6 Reported in *East Europe* for July 1957, p. 56. I borrow this reference from Sidney Hook, *Political Power and Personal Freedom*, New York, Collier, 1962, p. 147.

7 I collected this one myself from the Dar-es-Salaam press, the following day, 8 July 1967. Although Dar is scarcely one of Ian Fleming's 'exciting cities' I have no difficulty at all in understanding that and why those who have settled there even into penury not only do not want to be pushed about 'for their own advantage' but also hate the thought of returning to, by comparison, the excruciating boredom of a Tanzanian village.

8 See on this, in the French Revolution of 1789, J. L. Talmon, *The Origins of Totalitarian Democracy*, London, Secker & Warburg, 1952. When Lenin first developed his ideas for 'a party of a new type' he himself contrasted what has since come to be called 'democratic centralism' with genuine democratic control; which last phrase he then interpreted in our first sense. See his *What Is To Be Done?*, translated by S. V. Utechin and Patricia Utechin, London, Panther, 1970, pp. 163–4, 185–6; and compare my 'Russell on Bolshevism', in a forthcoming collection edited by George W. Roberts, to be published by Allen & Unwin.

9 A. de Tocqueville, *Democracy in America*, edited by Richard D. Heffner, New York, New American Library, 1956, part I, ch. III.

10 There is even one, Donald McIntyre — from the Labour Party of Ellen Wilkinson rather than that of Edward Short — who dares to argue 'that assessment — whether by written examinations or by other techniques — is an integral part of effective teaching' (*ED*, p. 164). He is still too modest, for there is, surely, a logically necessary connection between assessment of some sort and both intentional teaching and intentional learning. See 'Teaching and testing', in my *Sociology, Equality and Education*, London, Macmillan, 1976.

11 J. Dewey and E. Dewey, *Schools of Tomorrow*, New York and London, Dutton and Dent, 1915, pp. 303ff.

12 On the back cover of *ED*, after ' ". . . essential reading . . ." *The Times Educational Supplement*', and before an enthusiastic puff from Clyde Chitty (*Morning Star*), we read words from John Vaizey's review in the *Listener*: '. . . the egalitarian passion of these writers is a passion that relies in the main on hard, cold, realistic scholarship'.

Certainly there is 'egalitarian passion' in plenty. But there is also a great deal which equally certainly is not 'hard, cold, realistic scholarship'. For example: the two editors, after asserting that, 'Throughout history the middle and upper classes . . . have given to the working classes as little and as poor an education as possible', in support deploy only two quotations. One of the quotations does nothing to vindicate their denunciations. The other maintains, in one particular case, its flat contrary (p. 7). Again, Anthony Arblaster quotes a famous Austin paper, and then denounces Austin for failing to take points which, had Arblaster been willing to read only three more pages, he would have found there made by Austin himself (p. 36). And so on.

For further details of these and other manifestations of the ideals and illusions of Penguin Education, consult the work mentioned in note 10 above.

13 Some, for instance, being at bottom utilitarians, believe only because they judge that the marginal utility of additions is less the more anyone has already. See A. M. Quinton, *Utilitarian Ethics*, London, Macmillan, 1973, pp. 75—6; and compare C. Jencks, *Inequality*, London, Allen Lane, 1973, pp. 9—10.

14 One, at page 87, begins: 'The devotion of democracy to education is a familiar fact . . . a government resting on popular suffrage cannot be successful unless those who elect and who obey their governors are educated.' But this rationale is dismissed as superficial: '. . . there is a deeper explanation. A democracy is more than a form of government; it is primarily a mode of associated living, of conjoint communicated experience.' So Dewey proceeds, in terms quoted earlier in the text, to apply his official criteria, and to promise 'the breaking down of those barriers of class, race, and nationality which kept men from perceiving the full import of their activity'.

The other political references are equally uninterested. At page 260 Dewey writes: 'In what is termed politics, democratic social organization makes provision for this direct participation in control. . . .' If this raises the spirits of participatory democrats, they will certainly be both surprised and disappointed to learn that the sentence immediately preceding suggests that the 'free or voluntary' activity of control can, apparently, mean as little as people's inert concern about 'the ends that control their activity'; for that sentence reads: 'In the degree in which men have an active concern in the ends that control their activity, their activity becomes free or voluntary and loses its externally enforced and servile quality, *even though the physical aspect of* behaviour *remain the same*' (italics supplied).

It is a relief after this to read, on page 301, at the end of a paragraph on German philosophy: 'Political democracy, with its belief in the right of individual desire and purpose to take part in re-adapting even the fundamental constitution of society, was foreign to it.' Again, 'civic efficiency' is defined, on page 120, as involving 'ability to judge men and measures wisely and to take a determining part in making as well as obeying laws'.

15 'Equality and education', in B. Wilson (ed.), *Education, Equality and Society*, London, Allen & Unwin, 1975, pp. 119–20.

16 *Ibid.*, p. 119: italics original. Jencks, who is very clear that and why equality of opportunity cannot produce equality of outcome (*op. cit.*, p. 37), has a whole chapter on 'Inequality in cognitive skills'. It ends with a list of ways in which 'cognitive inequality' could or could not be reduced. Recognizing that this possible ideal might be achieved by arranging that the ablest children should have the least schooling and the dullest the most, Jencks himself stands up for what he calls 'equal opportunity' — eccentrically construed as 'implying that everyone should get as much schooling *as he wants*' (*ibid.*, p. 107: italics supplied). But, be warned now, if such cognitive inequality 'were a principal cause of inequality in other realms, this traditional doctrine might need re-examination' (*ibid.*, pp. 109–10).

17 Dewey does often think of scarce talents as a resource too precious to be left unexploited. For instance, in a chapter on 'Vocational aspects of education', he says: '. . . since slaves were confined to certain prescribed callings, much talent must have remained unavailable to the community, and hence there was a dead loss' (*DE*, pp. 308–9: and compare pp. 94, 118–19).

18 This conclusion is, surely, likely to be of practical relevance in a society such as ours which has had considerable social mobility for some time. Certainly we have no business simply to assume that the children either of every group of people or of every recognized social class must be on average in every respect as well or ill endowed as the children of every other group or class. Yet the Penguin Educationalist, Peter Mauger, like so many others, takes it that, if the children of one social class are below average in their performance under some system of selection for talent, then that fact is by itself sufficient to show that the system is inefficient, unfair, and ought to be abolished. It does not follow.

He begins: 'Research has shown beyond a shadow of a doubt that working-class children are grossly under-represented in grammar schools'; and he then gives a reference to work by J. W. B. Douglas. Mauger now proceeds immediately to his conclusion: 'These figures alone are strong enough arguments for the abolition of maintained grammar schools and direct grant schools. If, after all these years of experiment in selection procedures, they can't do better than this . . .' (*ED*, pp. 130–1).

19 Sidney Hook, *Education and the Taming of Power*, London, Alcove, 1974. The quality which Dewey took for granted is one which from personal knowledge I can say that Hook too possesses in abundance.

20 *Treatise*, III (ii) 2; page 490 in the Selby-Bigge edition, Oxford University Press, 1906.

Antony Flew

21 The useful expressions, 'high redefinition' and 'low redefinition', for those which, respectively, increase and reduce the required qualifications, were introduced by Paul Edwards in 'Bertrand Russell's doubts about induction', first published in *Mind*, 1949, and reprinted in Antony Flew (ed.), *Logic and Language*, Oxford, Blackwell, First Series, 1951.

22 *The Wealth of Nations*, IV (ii), p. 400, vol. 1, Everyman edition. Compare F. A. Hayek, 'The results of human action but not of human design', in his *Studies in Philosophy, Politics and Economics*, London, Routledge & Kegan Paul, 1967.

23 Dewey earlier contrasts indirect education, 'by direct sharing in the pursuits of grown-ups', with formal education, in 'Intentional agencies — schools'; warning that the latter 'easily becomes remote and dead' (*DE*, p. 8). I recall here a tale told by a former Ghanaian colleague. He was himself present at a Convention People's Party demonstration against the University of Ghana, at which the slogan was raised: 'Down with bookism!'

24 They became more so later. Hook claims to have played a part in this change: 'I had contended, and still do, that only in a democratic socialist economy in which housing, schooling and vocational opportunities are planned in relation to the needs of individuals, and not made dependent upon the vagaries of the market, could the educated ideals of *Democracy and Education* be realised. By the time he published his *Liberalism and Social Action* Dewey had come round to accepting this . . .' (*op. cit.*, p. 175).

It is clear that Hook was working on a subject already more than half converted, disinclined to criticize socialist ideas. For instance: Dewey asserts that employees cannot have 'insight into the social aims of their pursuits' unless the industries in which they work are under collective control. At present, he says, 'The results actually achieved are not the ends of *their* actions, but only of their employers' (*DE*, p. 260: italics original). Yet why on earth should anyone accept this contemptuous and doctrinaire contention, that people working in individually owned bakeries, plastics factories, or whatever else, cannot appreciate that the products of their work meet their own and other people's needs for these products?

25 J. Ratner (ed.), *Democracy in Education*, London, Allen & Unwin, 1941, p. 63.

26 *Principles of Political Economy*, V (xi). Those who have heard that Mill was a Fabian socialist before their time should study this whole chapter. It contains uninhibited Selsdon Group attacks on all monopolies, but especially state monopolies, as well as on excesses and abuses of trades union power. Compare my 'J. S. Mill: socialist or libertarian?', in M. Ivens (ed.), *Prophets of Freedom and Enterprise*, London, Kogan Page, 1975.

27 'One's self I sing', in E. de Selincourt (ed.), *Selected Poems*, Oxford University Press, 1920, p. 1.

28 'Song of myself', *ibid.*, p. 44.

29 'I was looking a long while', *ibid.*, p. 297.
30 'To foreign lands', *ibid.*, p. 3.

6   John Dewey's philosophy of education
R. S. Peters

Introduction

It would be tempting to regard John Dewey's philosophy of education as an extrapolation of key features of learning situations in the old rural life, in which he was nurtured, to schooling in the industrial society which developed during his lifetime. Dewey experienced the new schooling first-hand as a not very successful teacher and was appalled by the rote-learning, regimentation, and irrelevance to life that characterized so much that went on. His philosophy, it might be said, was an attempt to introduce into this new institution the problem-solving, do-it-yourself method of the learning of his boyhood, together with the close link between learning and living and the sense of contributing to a social whole permeated by shared experiences.

No doubt there is some truth in this suggestion; for people's views about an educational situation are very much influenced by early models which they encounter. Michael Oakeshott, for instance, confessed at the end of an article on 'Learning and teaching'[1] that he owed his recognition of the values of patience, accuracy, economy, elegance, and style to a sergeant gymnastics instructor, 'not on account of anything he said', but because he exemplified them.

The key to understanding Dewey's philosophy of education, however, is not just his early experience nor the obvious point that he was a pragmatist who applied the doctrines of Charles Peirce and William James in a straightforward way to education. Rather it is the realization that he was, for a long time, a Hegelian who *later* became converted to pragmatism. Dewey, like Hegel, could not tolerate dualisms. He had a passion for unifying doctrines that, on the surface, seemed irreconcilable. Pragmatism, and especially its emphasis on scientific method, together with categories of thought

extrapolated from biology, seemed to him the key to unification. It also seemed a natural extension of his early experiences
of problem-solving.

In his educational theory this passion for unification, for
getting rid of dualisms, had ample scope as the titles of his
books indicate: *The Child and the Curriculum,*[2] *The School
and Society,*[3] *Interest and Effort in Education,*[4] *Experience
and Education*[5] and so on. This quest for unity, which Dewey
substituted for the despised quest for certainty, explains why
Dewey was not a wholehearted supporter of the progressive
movement in America and ended up by writing his *Experience and Education*, which was highly critical of some of its
practices.

1 Individual growth and shared experiences

The exception might seem to be *Democracy and Education,*[6]
which is a puzzling book, for there is plenty about education
in it but very little about democracy — no proper discussion
of liberty, equality and the rule of law, no probing of the
problems of representation, participation, and the control of
the executive. The explanation of this is that Dewey viewed
democracy mainly as a way of life; he was not particularly
interested in the institutional arrangements necessary to support it. This way of life, he claimed, had two main features.
First, it was characterized by numerous and varied shared
interests and concerns. These play an important role in social
control. Second, there is full and free interaction between
social groups, with plenty of scope for communication.[7] This
is surely a strange characterization of democracy. What is
significant about it, however, is the emphasis on the social.
Dewey later says:[8]

> And the idea of perfecting an 'inner' personality is a sure
> sign of social divisions. What is called inner is simply that
> which does not connect with others — which is not capable
> of free and full communication. What is termed spiritual
> culture has usually been futile, with something rotten about
> it, just because it has been conceived as a thing which a
> man might have internally — and therefore exclusively.

103

> What one is as a person is what one is as associated with
> others, in a free give and take of intercourse.

There is nothing particularly surprising about this view of
Dewey's background in idealism. Indeed it is very reminiscent
of Bradley's attack on individualism in his famous chapter on
'My station and its duties'.[9] Also the distinction between the
public and the private has never been so sharply drawn in
American society as in Europe. A modern symptom of this
is that in a typical American township they have no walls to
their gardens. But the puzzle is to reconcile this emphasis on
'shared experiences' and social approval and disapproval, as
one of the main moulders of character, which Dewey empha-
sizes, with his view of education as individual growth.

Much has been written about the unsatisfactoriness of this
biological metaphor which Dewey used to impose unity on
his theorizing. He argued that growth does not have an end
but *is* an end. Thus education is not necessarily a matter of
age; for education means the enterprise of supplying the conditions which ensure growth, or adequacy of life, irrespective
of age. Living has its own intrinsic quality, whether in youth
or in maturity, and the business of education is with that
quality.

But, it is usually objected, how can 'growth' provide
criteria of this quality? Did not Napoleon or the Marquis de
Sade 'grow'? Dewey faced this problem in *Experience and
Education*[10] and argued that growth in efficiency as a burglar,
as a gangster, or as a corrupt politician does not lead to further growth. Growth in general is retarded by such limited
forms of growth. This answer did not help him much as many
have pointed out, with imaginative sketches of the developing life-styles of burglars, train robbers, etc. What he needed
was other criteria by reference to which desirable and undesirable forms of growth could be distinguished.

In actual fact I think that Dewey *did* have other criteria of
value for education. His metaphor of 'growth', like his other
concepts of 'interaction' and 'continuity', are just part of his
conceptual apparatus, taken from biology, which symbolize
his insistence that man is part of the natural world. He could
not tolerate the dualism, found in thinkers such as Kant and

Descartes, between man and nature any more than he could tolerate other dualisms. But later in *Democracy and Education*[11] he reached what he called a 'technical definition' of 'education' as 'that reconstruction or re-organization of experiences which adds to the meaning of experience, and which increases ability to direct the course of subsequent experience'. He went on to say that an activity which brings education or instruction with it makes one aware of some of the *connections* which had been imperceptible. He stressed the addition in *knowledge* both of the child who reaches for a bright light and gets burned and of the scientist learning more about fire in his laboratory. In brief, Dewey's main concern was with growth in practical *knowledge*, in the development of critical intelligence as described in his earlier popular book *How We Think*.[12]

But Dewey, as a pragmatist, was also interested in what he called 'the other side of an educative experience' which is the 'added power of direction or control'. He contrasted this with aimless activity, on the one hand, and he singled out acting under external direction as a classic example of this, and routine activity on the other hand, which only increases skill in doing a particular thing. This could be interpreted as a way of stressing the virtue of autonomy, of self-initiated action which is the outcome of independent thought. Indeed, Dr Dearden, in his *The Philosophy of Primary Education*,[13] sees autonomy as the ethical value which is embedded in the whole growth ideology. What is common to both is the notion of self-originated activity. This is certainly a valid interpretation of many other more individualistic theorists who made use of the metaphor of 'growth'. But I doubt whether it completely fits Dewey with his continued emphasis on 'shared experiences' and communication. I think his ideal was much more that of a group of dedicated, problem-solving scientists, who were united by their shared concerns and willingness to communicate their findings to each other. The 'lonely will' of the individual was anathema to him,[14] though in chapter 5 of *Experience and Education* he does extol the virtue of 'freedom' understood as self-control whilst pointing out that too much freedom understood negatively as the absence of social constraints may be destructive of shared co-operative activities. I think that he more or less took for granted the value of individual self-determination but was more concerned to stress the values of *co-operative* problem-solving as an antidote to the extremes of individualism in the old pioneer period.

This interpretation of Dewey's concept of education not only gives more determinateness to his somewhat nebulous metaphor of 'growth'; it also explains the link which he forged between education and his rather strange conception of the democratic way of life. His emphasis, in the latter, on numerous shared interests and communication makes sense if it is seen as a projection of features of the kinds of communities in which he worked and lived, for Dewey was an academic who, as well as writing forty books and about 700 articles, was constantly founding and joining groups concerned with various forms of social and educational reform. Thus growth for him was not growth in *any* direction which would be consistent with his claim that desirable growth is that which permits more growth; it is rather growth in practical critical thought, which opens up the possibility of more control of the environment. But this is not something which the individual does on his own. In his early days at Michigan one of Dewey's colleagues was G. H. Mead, whose theories about the social nature of the self and the social determinants of thought influenced Dewey profoundly. These theories strengthened Dewey's Hegelian convictions about the social nature of man and supplied support for his own distinctive brand of pragmatism, with its emphasis on 'shared experiences'. It enabled him to argue that growth, properly understood, can only flourish in a democratic environment. Indeed, to use a Platonic metaphor, for Dewey the democratic way of life is growth 'writ large'. There is unity discernible beneath the appearances of democracy and education.

2 Individual interest and external direction

Dewey's attempt to transcend dualisms is nowhere more apparent than in his treatment of the teaching situation.

(i) Aims of education

There is first of all his treatment of aims of education in which he attacked the false dichotomy between means and ends which he exposed at greater length in his *Human Nature and Conduct*.[15] But he had additional concerns in his educational writings. First, he insisted on the intrinsic value of educational activities. They are not merely unavoidable means to something else.[16] Second, he maintained that good aims arise from what is going on, from the purposes of the pupil. They must not be externally imposed, or ready made. Nevertheless he did not advocate a kind of free for all in which *any* aims are accepted if they arise in this way. They must be capable of translation into a method of co-operating with those undergoing instruction; they must lend themselves to the construction of specific procedures. And who is to be the judge of this unless it is the teacher? Also Dewey realized that such aims do not spring spontaneously from the nature of the child. Indeed, he criticized Rousseau for making Nature his God. They are moulded by what he called 'the social medium'. Although he was critical of imitation as an important factor in 'the social medium' he admitted the large influence of social approval and disapproval.[17] Thus all along the line Dewey tried to combine the progressive child-centred approach with what he had learnt from Mead and with what was in his bones as a Hegelian. He resisted external *direction* and *imposition* but insisted on the importance of external approval and encouragement. He thus achieved some kind of reconciliation between the progressive and traditional views of teaching.

(ii) Teaching methods

This attempt to get rid of dualisms was made even more explicit in his *Experience and Education*.[18] He was at pains to point out that he was not suggesting a passive or spectatorial role for the teacher. Indeed, he argued that 'basing education upon personal experience may mean more multiplied and more intimate contacts between the mature and the immature than ever existed in the traditional school, and consequently

more rather than less guidance by others'.[19] In their account
of Dewey's laboratory school Mayhew and Edwards insist
that 'Those planning the activities must see each child as an
ever changing person. . . . They must carefully select and
grade the materials used, altering such selection, as is necessary in all experimentation. . . .'[20] (This was practicable
because of the extremely favourable teacher-pupil ratio. The
school started with 3 regular teachers for 32 children; rose to
16 teachers for 60 children, and ended with 23 teachers plus
10 assistants for 140 children!)

Dewey himself described this careful grading and selection
of material in terms of his two criteria of educative experiences, 'interaction' and 'continuity'. He used the term 'interaction', rather than more homely terms such as 'needs' and
'purposes' of the child, not purely because of his desire to
create some kind of biological unity between the processes
of education and those of life but also because too many progressives, in his opinion, had neglected the objective conditions of situations and the role of the teacher in arranging
for them to match the internal conditions of the child. Similarly 'continuity' was stressed because it was not sufficient
for the child to be interested in anything; interests had to be
explored which were rich in possibilities for future experiences. So 'guidance' by the teacher was substituted for the
'external direction' of traditional methods, and because
interests arose from the child, deriving from his 'impulses' of
investigation and experimentation, constructiveness, expres-
siveness and the social impulse,[21] the approach could claim
to be child-centred.

The method of learning which conformed to these criteria of 'educative experiences' was that of problem-solving,
a detailed account of which was given by Dewey in *How
We Think*. This stress on problem-solving as a method was
later taken up by Kilpatrick and formalized in the project
method. Dewey was favourably disposed towards it but
did not become a passionate advocate of it. To be fair to
him he was always very guarded about details of teaching methods. He confined himself to generalities, knowing that details of implementation must vary with individuals.

(iii) Social control and the role of the teacher

Dewey's account of the social control of the teacher exhibited the same tendency towards unification. He tried to transcend the dichotomy between the 'keeping order' view of the traditional school and the self-imposed discipline advocated by the progressives. He compared children in a classroom to their participation in a game. Games involve rules and children do not feel that they are submitting to external imposition in obeying them. The control of the actions of the participating individuals is affected by the whole situation in which individuals are involved, in which they share and of which they are co-operative or interacting parts.

The teacher exercises authority in such a situation as the representative and agent of the interests of the group as a whole. If he or she has to take firm action it is done on behalf of the interests of the group, not as an exhibition of personal power. In the traditional school the teacher had to 'keep order' because order was in the teacher's keeping instead of residing in the shared work being done. In the new schools the main job of the teacher is to think and plan ahead so that knowledge of individuals may be married with knowledge of subject-matter that will enable activities to be selected which lend themselves to social organization. Thus 'the teacher loses the position of external boss or dictator but takes on that of leader of group activities'.[22]

3 The content of education and the role of the school

Dewey is sometimes classified with those progressives who have extolled following the interests of the child at the expense of subject-matter. This is completely to misunderstand his position, for he was too much of a Hegelian to ignore the importance of a society's 'cultural heritage' which he described as 'the ripe fruitage of experience'. But, again as a Hegelian, he strove to remove the dichotomy between both 'the child' and 'the curriculum', and 'the school' and 'society'. On the one hand, therefore, he insisted that the curriculum should embody what he called the sociological and the psychological principles. The sociological principle demanded that the pupil be initiated into the customs, habits, values, and knowledge which constitute the culture of a community. The psychological principle demanded that this should be done with due regard to the pupil's individual needs, interests and problems.

On the other hand he believed passionately that the curriculum should be socially relevant. It should contribute to making children active members of a democratic society. Indeed, on this theme Dewey waxed almost mystical and poetic:[23]

> When the school introduces and trains each child of society into membership within such a little community, saturating him with the spirit of service, and providing him with the instruments of effective self-direction, we shall have the deepest and best guarantee of a larger society, which is worthy, lovely and harmonious.

Let us, therefore, consider in more detail his resolution of the dichotomies between the child and the curriculum and between the school and society.

(i) The child and the curriculum

Most of what Dewey wrote about the curriculum related to the elementary school and much of it seems rather dated. But it illustrates well his approach. He stressed, first of all, the importance of practical activities such as sewing, cooking, weaving, carpentry and metalwork. These conformed to the sociological principle because they were basic to life, being concerned with food, clothing, etc., and thus part of the cultural heritage. They also conformed to the psychological principle for two reasons. First, Dewey was convinced that children are interested in them. Second, they embody motor activities which Dewey considered to be closely connected with mental development as a whole. Also, from an educational point of view, they were capable of providing continuity in that they could open up all sorts of other fruitful studies. As he put it: 'You can concentrate the history of all mankind into the evolution of the flax, cotton and wool fibres into clothing.'[24]

In addition to practical activities he included some traditional 'subjects' in the curriculum with the proviso that they
should be related to his concept of man as a problem-solving
animal concerned with control over his environment. Thus he
regarded geography as being of particular importance – but
as a way of gaining in power to perceive the spatial, the
natural connections of an ordinary act. History was acceptable, too, as a way of recognizing the human connections of
ordinary acts.[25] And both, of course, must start from the
child's immediate interests – geography must move outwards
from local geography and history from 'some present situation with its problems'.[26] Science is, of course, included, but
subject to the same sort of provisos. It should be taught with
the psychological principle in mind and start from the everyday experience of the learner. There was too much of a tendency to teach it in the logical order of the developed study.
Above all, science should be taught as the agency of progress
in action, for it opens up new ends as well as helping mankind
to achieve existing ones. Because of science man can now
'face the future with a firm belief that intelligence properly
used can do away with evils once thought inevitable'.[27]

Finally the curriculum should include communication
skills such as reading, writing, mathematics, and foreign languages. These appealed to the child's 'impulses' to express
himself and to share his experiences with others. So the best
time to teach him the techniques of communication is when
the need to communicate is vitally important to him. These
communication skills should be taught incidentally as the
need arose.

(ii) The school and society

There were two aspects of Dewey's attempt to resolve the
dualism between the school and society. The first dealt with
the relationship of the school to the home and surrounding
community, the second with its relationship to the wider
society which the pupil would enter on leaving school. On
the first aspect, as I said at the beginning, Dewey was greatly
impressed by the informal type of learning that went on in
the home and in the small rural communities that were

passing. He frequently contrasted this natural way of learning, in which there was no separation between learning and life, with the artificial drills and recitations of formal schooling. His plea was that there should be an indissoluble link between learning in school and learning out of school.[28] Dewey's insistence that the school itself should be a real community, exhibiting numerous shared interests and open communication, was his answer to the other question of the school's relationship to the wider society. The school itself should be a miniature democracy, according to his understanding of 'democracy'. He saw this type of school not only as valuable in itself, because of the quality of life that it made possible, but also as the springboard to social progress. Dewey took a prominent part in the current controversy about Trade Schools and vocational education.[29] He deprecated, of course, the split between the practical and the liberal which reflected an undesirable type of class-structure. He objected to the implicit suggestion that education should be made subservient to the demands of interested manufacturers. Nevertheless his solution was typically one in which the dualism between vocational and liberal education could be resolved; for he argued that if more practical activities were introduced into schools, education would be *through* occupations and not *for* occupations. He advocated the introduction of processes involved in industrial life to make school life more active, more impregnated with science, and more in touch with the world. This should be part of *everybody's* education, not just a special provision for those who were singled out to become the modern equivalents of hewers of wood and drawers of water. Above all, a different attitude to work should be developed so that young people would become imbued with a sense of community service instead of working only for private gain. It should 'train power of readaptation to changing conditions so that future workers would not become blindly subject to a fate imposed upon them'.[30]

4 General comments

What is to be made of this intellectual edifice? For opinions about it are very varied. I once tried to get an eminent

112

American philosopher interested in the philosophy of education. He grunted and remarked that John Dewey had set that
subject up — and killed it stone dead! On the other hand
Sidney Hook, another eminent American philosopher, published a book as recently as 1973, in which he included several
essays in defence of Dewey.[31] He saw Dewey's philosophy as
providing a middle road between radicals such as Reimer,
Goodman and Illich, and the post-sputnik traditionalists such
as Vice-Admiral Rickover. I agree with Sidney Hook that
such a middle road is necessary, but I do not find the one
signposted by Dewey particularly convincing or congenial;
for his way of resolving various dualisms by his account of
the 'growth' of the problem-solving man has the character of
a panacea which involves both distortion in the sphere of
what he called the sociological principle and a romantic ideali-
zation in the sphere of the psychological principle. The dualisms are not in fact resolved. Let me explain these criticisms
before addressing myself to an estimate of his unifying ideal.

(i) The sociological principle

Dewey admitted the importance of making the child aware of
his cultural heritage but only on the condition that he should
be introduced to it in a way which stressed its relevance to
present practical and social problems. This is understandable
as said against unimaginative rote-learning of classical textbooks, but, if taken seriously, is a good recipe for failing to
understand what we have inherited, for it fails to take
account of the degree of autonomy which some traditions of
inquiry have from contemporary practical problems. Understanding depends upon entering imaginatively into the mind
of those who have contributed to these traditions and grasp-
ing what their problems were as arising from them. Copernicus
and Kepler, for instance, were both working within the
Pythagorean tradition. The heliocentric theory emerged because it was mathematically simpler; Kepler's second law of
planetary motion was lighted on in the course of speculations
about the music of the heavenly bodies. To stress the relevance of these momentous advances for navigation or space
travel does nothing towards understanding them as theories.

113

R. S. Peters

It may be said that the point is not so much to understand such theories thoroughly, but to use them. But a failure to understand properly the problems with which people in the past have been concerned often leads to absurdities in attempts to use them. Piaget, for instance, was greatly influenced by Kant. Piaget's theories are widely applied in the educational sphere in a ham-handed way because the educationalist in question has no conception of what Kant was about in his critiques. The school, surely, should not concern itself only with what is relevant to contemporary problems. It should *also* distance itself a bit from these and introduce children to speculations about the world in science, and to insights into the human condition in literature and history, which are of perennial significance. The dualism is there and gives rise to continuing tensions.

Dewey's view of the teacher, who is society's agent for the transmission and development of its cultural heritage, is also unsatisfactory, for it slurs over the dualism between the teacher's position as an authority and the legitimate demand for 'participation'. A teacher is not just a leader in a game, like a football captain. In a game most of the participants know how to play; but pupils come to a teacher because they are ignorant, and he or she is meant to be, to some extent, an authority on some aspect of the culture. This disparity between teacher and taught — especially in the primary school — makes talk of 'democracy in education' problematic, unless 'democracy' is watered down to mean just multiplying shared experiences and openness of communication, as by Dewey. If 'democracy' is to include, as it usually does, some suggestion of participation in decision-making, we are then confronted with current tensions underlying the question of how much 'participation' is compatible with the freedom and authority of the teacher.

Dewey himself never paid much attention to institutional issues. This was not just because he lived before the days when 'participation' became an issue. It was also because his attitude towards the democratic way of life was semi-mystical. 'When the emotional force, the mystical force, one might say, of the miracles of the shared life and shared experience is spontaneously felt, the hardness and concreteness of contem-

114

porary life will be bathed in a light that never was on land or sea.'[32] I wonder if he always felt like this about sitting on committees!

(ii) The psychological principle

Dewey's treatment of the psychological principle was equally unsatisfactory; for it combined a conception of the child, which was almost as idealistic as his conception of democracy, with a too limited view of what he called 'the social medium'. This led him to oversimplify the dualism between what he called 'internal conditions' and what is the result of social influences. Dewey was impressed, as I have reiterated, by the informal learning that went on in the home and in the local community and wanted to forge a link between this sort of learning and learning at school. But he did not ask the questions 'which home?' and 'which local community?', for sociologists have catalogued the vast disparities that exist between homes in this respect.

Dewey's account of the ideal educational situation assumed, to start with, an 'impulse' to investigate and experiment, as well as a 'social impulse' from which co-operation stems. Maybe most of the children in his Laboratory School had such impulses. Maybe all children have them at birth. But by the time they get to school it is noticeable how many children seem to lack these 'impulses' — and this is probably due to the *absence* of eager learning at home. Second, as Dewey pointed out, there may not be much potentiality for 'growth' in some problem which actually bothers a child. So the teacher must try to divert him on to some other problem. Teachers come to know from experience, on the grapevine, or from books, which topics present rich possibilities for a project. So those going round schools find that, miraculously, children in many different schools seem to be bothered about water, costume, or flight! So projects can become as standardized and externally imposed as straightforward instruction.

This, on a broader view than Dewey's, is not a damaging objection to the use of projects and the problem-solving method generally; for one of the gifts of the teacher is to stimulate interest and to get pupils to regard as problematic

115

situations which they never previously viewed in this light. What Dewey called 'interaction' is not just a function of *existing* 'internal conditions' within the pupil. There is the problem, too, that if existing 'internal conditions' are taken as seriously as the desirability of co-operation, a highly individualized curriculum would be the result which would require something like the very favourable teacher-pupil ratio of the Dewey school and which might also mean that many pupils end up with vast gaps in their knowledge.

The same idealistic outlook is evident in Dewey's treatment of the problem of social control, which, for many teachers nowadays, is a constant source of strain. When talking of the problem of unruly children Dewey remarks that: 'There are likely to be some who, when they come to school, are already victims of injurious conditions outside of the school.'[33] But this does not apply just to odd individuals; it applies also to a vast multitude of children who come to school with an attitude towards learning which makes it very difficult for the teacher to contrive a situation in the classroom that approximates to a game in which they eagerly participate. Similarly the one thing which they expect of the teacher is that he or she will be able to 'keep order'. The attitude towards authority, which is determined by the control system of their homes, makes it very difficult for them to take seriously a teacher who regards himself or herself just as a friendly guide presiding to ensure continuity in their shared experiences of problem-solving. It takes a very skilful teacher to resocialize such children so that they are ready to learn in the way in which Dewey approved. I mention this rather mundane criticism because I do not think Dewey conceived of himself as putting forward an ideal which could only be realized in a school like his own Laboratory School, which catered for children whose home backgrounds were rich in experience and favourable towards learning. His message was that the school could transform society; so I think he thought that this type of learning situation could be generalized straight away. It is at this point that my scepticism grows.

Another defect in Dewey's treatment of the 'social medium' and of his slurring over the dualism between the child's 'internal conditions' and what he gets from others is his dismissal of imitation as being of much importance.[34] If this is extended to include identification it can work both negatively and positively for the teacher. The negative aspect is that so many of the models in society, with whom children identify, are anti-educational from Dewey's point of view. He always argued that education provides its own ends; it is not merely a means to money, prestige or a good job. Yet the child is constantly presented with models of people who have got on in the world. The questions 'What is the pay off?' or 'Where does this get you?' are asked about almost anything. It is very tempting, therefore, for the teacher to make use of extrinsic motivations such as marks, prizes, competition, etc., perhaps refined by Skinnerian techniques, in order to get children to learn, for, because of the ethos of individualistic societies, and the models which they throw up, these forms of motivation are readily understood. Co-operating with others in shared experiences because of their intrinsic value has not, unfortunately, the same straightforward appeal.

On the positive side, however, imitation and identification can work for the teacher if he or she has mastery of and enthusiasm for what is being taught. A good example of this is the case of Oakeshott and the sergeant gymnastics instructor mentioned at the start. Dewey, I suspect, was hostile to imitation because it smacks of external imposition. But it is rather cavalier for a thinker with an evolutionary orientation like Dewey to disregard one of the main mechanisms which the human race has evolved for the transmission of culture. Bronfenbrenner, for instance, in his *Two Worlds of Childhood*,[35] contrasts the USA and USSR from the point of view of the degree to which systematic modelling is encouraged. His chapter on 'The unmaking of the American child' makes very sobering reading.

Dewey was well aware of the features of industrial society that were inimical to his whole conception of democracy and of education. In his *Individualism, Old and New*[36] he pointed out the irrelevance of the old individualistic values that had characterized the pioneer; for the present problem was not that of wrestling with physical nature but that of dealing with social conditions. Earlier individualism had shrunk to industrial initiative and ability in making money. This was the main enemy. What was needed was a *new* individualism. Dewey refrained from sketching what it would be like but suggested that technology, taken in its broadest sense, offers the main clue to its nature, for it would help both to transform society and to develop a new type of individual mind.

(iii) The technological man

What, then, is to be the verdict on Dewey's ideal of the technological, problem-solving man which is central to understanding his convictions about the methods and content of education and his conception of democracy? Surely what was said of Bernard Shaw: 'He is like the Venus de Milo. What there is of him is admirable.'

There are two respects in which Dewey's ideal speaks very much to our condition. First, the plea for the use of practical intelligence, backed up by the use of science, to tackle social and economic problems, is as pertinent today as it was at the time at which he was writing. Second, his emphasis on 'shared experiences' and communication and his attack on the relics of the old individualism are apposite in a society dominated by frustration of the desire for material gain. We could do with more fraternity, the forgotten ideal of the French Revolution. But he was mistaken in thinking that the ideals of individualism have shrunk just to the desire for profit. There are also autonomy, integrity, and authenticity which are still potent individualistic ideals both in life and in education. His playing down of such ideals is surprising; for they can scarcely be dismissed as facets of the 'rottenness' of perfecting an inner personality. He says of aims of education that we do not emphasize things which do not require emphasis. He may well have thought this about such individualistic ideals, though I suspect that he did not.

(a) Neglect of the personal and of the education of the emotions

What, then, are the defects of this ideal? Mainly that, rather ironically, in putting forward an ideal which is meant to resolve current dualisms, he develops a very onesided view of man that completely ignores certain features of the human condition. First, Dewey ignores the purely personal life of

human beings. By that I don't mean just his failure to emphasize the importance of respect for persons in his account of
democracy, nor his attack on the 'rottenness' of individual
attempts at self-improvement; I mean also his neglect of
interpersonal relationships and the education of the emotions.
It is significant that he makes practically no mention of the
role of literature in education. Literature is singularly un-
amenable to the problem-solving method of learning, and
often concerns itself with the predicaments of man rather
than with his problems. I once attended a poetry lesson in an
American school. The teacher read part of Gray's 'Elegy'
beautifully and then opened up a somewhat desultory discussion on what a curfew was, etc. I asked her why she did not
read it again as she had such a lovely voice and had the pupils
spellbound. 'Oh,' she said, 'we are only allowed to read it
once. It is meant to provide material for discussion and
problem-solving to help the children to become democratic
citizens.' She was surely echoing John Dewey's ideology.

(b) Predicaments as well as problems   This brings me to the
second comment on Dewey's ideal — the emphasis on problem-
solving. He shared the view of most Americans of that period
that life presented mainly problems that could be solved,
given the time and the technology. This optimism is of course
waning somewhat, in the face of the intractability of problems connected with race, unemployment, and poverty. But
even if it were not, the view of life presented is onesided, not
to say *exhausting*. Dewey, of course, appreciated the importance of habit in life, but accorded no value to anything that
was a matter of routine. Yet there is nothing particularly
wicked about the conservative pleasures derived from repeti-
tion and familiarity. There are also the more distanced,
aesthetic enjoyments that have little to do with problem-
solving. There are many aspects of life, too, that present not
problems that can be solved but predicaments that have to be
lived with. If a man in his prime is afflicted by a coronary or
loses his wife, he does not just have a problem.

(c) Disregard of the irrational   The third criticism is like the
second in that it is directed against Dewey's confident,

R. S. Peters

reformist optimism. He completely ignores the fundamental irrationality of man. He never mentions Freud, who was a contemporary of his, and seems sublimely unaware of the diagnosis of the human condition that derived from his insights. The view that civilization is a brittle crust containing with difficulty irrational yearnings, made no impact on Dewey in spite of his active interest in the rise of Nazism as a threat to democracy[37] — and what a limited perspective on Nazism!

(d) Defects of the pragmatic stance   There are finally the defects of Dewey's pragmatic stance. Others have commented in detail on the defects of the pragmatic theory of truth.[38] I shall confine myself to more general issues, which are crucial to his educational ideal. Basically the pragmatist lacks reverence, is guilty of what Russell calls 'cosmic impiety'.[39] He sees nature just as something that can be used for human purposes. He lacks a sense of awe and of wonder. This is manifest, too, in Dewey's insistence that history and geography must be taught subject to the condition that they throw light on contemporary problems and concerns. There is no reason why these should not be used as a starting point if they are motivationally potent, but to view such studies *only* under this aspect is both to distort them and to encourage a kind of present-centred ὕβρις.

It is the same with science. Dewey actually grossly exaggerated the connection between scientific theories and everyday practical problems. But to represent scientific theories, which are some of the greatest products of the human imagination, just as aids to action, is to ignore a whole dimension of human life. His psychology is made to fit this emphasis; for the child is credited with an 'impulse' to investigate and experiment but not with a more generalized 'drive to know' with which modern psychologists credit even monkeys. So Dewey put into the child at the beginning in the form of 'impulses' what he took out at the end in the form of the co-operative, communicative, technological man. The dimensions of speculative curiosity, of wonder and awe, are missing.

I am not of course suggesting that technology is unimportant in comparison with disinterested speculation. Still less

120

am I suggesting that 'relevance' is an unimportant criterion of learning and of the curriculum. What I am suggesting is that Dewey's ideal is as myopic as his conception of 'relevance'. Contributing to practical purposes is only *one* criterion of 'relevance'. The others are not limited to that which arouses plain curiosity; there are also countless studies in literature, religion, history, psychology, and the social sciences which are of great *emotional* significance to human beings without being obviously connected with practical purposes. When Whitehead said that education is the 'acquisition of the art of the utilization of knowledge'[40] I'm sure that he did not think of 'utilization' purely in terms of relevance to practical purposes. What he meant was that the content of education should have *application* to people's lives. It should not consist in 'inert ideas' propounded by teachers on the assumption that their pupils are going to be devotees of their subject like themselves — for one of the crucial questions for any teacher is what there is in his subject for the majority who are unlikely to become specialists in it.

(e) Conclusion To sum up: Dewey's revolt against the formalism and irrelevance of much that went on in schools is still pertinent. So is his plea for more 'shared experiences' and more development of practical intelligence. But his ideal of the technological man is too limited and culture bound. It ignores whole dimensions of the human condition — especially the predicaments of man, his irrationality, and his emotional sensitivities and susceptibilities. The cult of co-operative action is a welcome antidote to the lonely quest for salvation or for private profit. But human beings inhabit a personal as well as a public world; they are circumscribed by a Nature that has to be accepted as well as transformed, that should be an object of enjoyment, of wonder and of awe as well as material to be mastered for human purposes. A balance has to be struck between personal preoccupations and public policies, between servile humility and masterful ὕβρις. These are dualisms that Dewey did *not* resolve.

121

R. S. Peters

Notes

My thanks are due to my colleagues, Pat White and Robert Dearden, for their helpful comments on a first revision of this paper.
 1 Oakeshott, M., 'Learning and teaching', in R. S. Peters (ed.), *The Concept of Education*, Routledge & Kegan Paul, London, 1967.
 2 Dewey, J., *The Child and the Curriculum*, University of Chicago Press, 1902.
 3 Dewey, J., *The School and Society*, University of Chicago Press, 1900; rev. eds, 1915, 1943.
 4 Dewey, J., *Interest and Effort in Education*, Houghton Mifflin, Boston, 1913.
 5 Dewey, J., *Experience and Education*, Macmillan, New York, 1938.
 6 Dewey, J., *Democracy and Education*, Macmillan, New York, 1916.
 7 *Ibid.*, ch. VII.
 8 *Ibid.*, p. 143.
 9 Bradley, F. H., *Ethical Studies*, Oxford University Press, 1876, ch. V.
10 *Op. cit.*
11 *Op. cit.*, pp. 89–90.
12 Dewey, J., *How We Think*, Heath, Boston, 1910.
13 Dearden, R. F., *The Philosophy of Primary Education*, Routledge & Kegan Paul, London, 1968.
14 Murdoch, I., *The Sovereignty of Good*, Routledge & Kegan Paul, London, 1970.
15 Dewey, J., *Human Nature and Conduct*, Henry Holt, New York, 1922.
16 Dewey, J., *Democracy and Education*, Macmillan, New York, 1916, p. 127.
17 *Ibid.*, pp. 41–2.
18 *Op. cit.*
19 *Ibid.*, p. 21.
20 Mayhew, K. C. and Edwards, A. C., *The Dewey School*, Atherton Press, New York, 1966, p. 22.
21 *Ibid.*, pp. 46, 41.
22 Dewey, J., *Experience and Education*, Macmillan, New York, 1938, p. 59.
23 Dewey, J., *The School and Society*, University of Chicago Press, 7th impression, 1963, p. 29.
24 *Ibid.*, p. 22.
25 Dewey, J., *Democracy and Education*, Macmillan, New York, 1916, p. 246.
26 *Ibid.*, p. 251.
27 *Ibid.*, p. 263.
28 Dewey, J., *The School and Society*, University of Chicago Press, 7th impression, 1963, p. 91.
29 Dykhuizen, G., *The Life and Mind of John Dewey*, Southern Illinois University Press, 1973, pp. 141–3.

30 Dewey, J., *Democracy and Education*, Macmillan, New York, 1916,
    p. 372.
31 Hook, S., *Education and the Taming of Power*, Open Court, New
    York, 1973.
32 Dewey, J., *Reconstruction in Philosophy*, Henry Holt, New York,
    1920, p. 211.
33 Dewey, J., *Experience and Education*, Macmillan, New York, 1938,
    p. 56.
34 Dewey, J., *Democracy and Education*, Macmillan, New York, 1916,
    pp. 40–3.
35 Bronfenbrenner, U., *Two Worlds of Childhood*, Allen & Unwin,
    London, 1971.
36 Dewey, J., *Individualism, Old and New*, Minton, Baker, New York,
    1936.
37 *See* Dykhuizen, *op. cit.*, pp. 240–1.
38 *See*, for instance, I. Scheffler, *Four Pragmatists*, Routledge & Kegan
    Paul, London, 1974.
39 Russell, B., *A History of Western Philosophy*, Allen & Unwin,
    London, 1946, p. 856.
40 Whitehead, A. N., *The Aims of Education*, Macmillan, London,
    1921; reprinted Mentor Books, USA, 1949, p. 16.

Index

Note: *the index does not include authors of works referred to only in bibliographical references*